BIOCIRCUITS

What People Are Saying About
Biocircuits:
Amazing New Tools for Energy Health

This book is a fascinating exploration of a whole new way of balancing the energies of the human body. It is a thorough presentation of both theory and personal experience. I have found biocircuits to be very valuable stress-reduction tools and a good adjunct to body work.
> —Joseph Heller,
> Creator of Hellerwork

A well-written eye-opener on the most exciting field in science today—the study of the body's electrical and quasi-electrical energy. This book offers more than abstract theory. It is an opportunity to experiment and experience results in your exploration of your body's subtle energy fields.
> —Michael Hutchison, Author, *MegaBrain*

A breakthrough tool for relieving biophysical stress! For a natural, non-medical modality, biocircuits can be remarkably powerful in producing quick, deep relaxation. This book is not just a lively and readable "how-to" book, it is a definitive introduction of a new subfield in the life-energy sciences.
> —Lee Sannella, MD, Psychiatrist, Researcher,
> and Author, *The Kundalini Experience*

Biocircuits can correct energy imbalances, sometimes dramatically. For instance, I have seen copper biocircuits actually double the speed at which the Qi flows through the energy meridians.
> —Miki Shima, OMD, CA, President,
> Japanese-American Acupuncture Foundation,
> Director, California Acupuncture Association

I like this book very much, and I can corroborate much of what it says. Biocircuits increase the flow of energies through the spine and balance the body's electropotentials. When you do this, you not only affect the physical body, but also help people mentally and emotionally, sometimes producing results that wouldn't be available with any other approach.
> —Jack Schwarz, Author, *Voluntary Controls,*
> *Human Energy Systems*

In my work in somatic psychotherapy, I've found biocircuits to be very useful in overcoming the resistance to translation from conceptual understanding to direct biophysical experience.

> —Robert K. Hall, MD, Founder and Director,
> Lomi School, Tomales School of Psychotherapy

This book is the most exciting and stimulating work on holistic health that I have seen in many years. . . . Everybody interested in maximum wellness should read it!

> —Robert Anton Wilson, Author, *The Cosmic Trigger,*
> *The Illuminati Trilogy*

Biocircuits really work, and they're easy and fun to use. In fact, these are the best natural tools I know to balance the total person and deepen consciousness for inner exploration. The Pattens have written the definitive work on an important, and hitherto little-known, technology.

> —Greg Neilsen, Author, *Pendulum Power, Pyramid Power*

Biocircuits are an idea whose time has finally come. Leslie and Terry Patten have performed a valuable service by bringing to light the important biocircuitry research of Eeman, Lindemann, and others.

> —Richard Gerber, MD, Author, *Vibrational Medicine*

$E = MC^2$ has far-reaching personal implications for all of us. *Biocircuits* explains why. More than that, it shows you how you can benefit from Einstein's discovery: It introduces a simple, practical way of learning for yourself that your body is energy, and that you can harness that energy to a significant degree for your health and psychic well-being. A most enjoyable and helpful book that should be in all public libraries.

> —George Feuerstein, Author, writing in *Spectrum Review*

BIOCIRCUITS

AMAZING NEW TOOLS FOR ENERGY HEALTH

**LESLIE
PATTEN**
With
**TERRY
PATTEN**

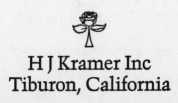

H J Kramer Inc
Tiburon, California

To our parents.

Published by H J Kramer Inc
P.O. Box 1082
Tiburon, CA 94920

ISBN 0-915811-13-8
Library of Congress Catalog Card Number: 88-081720

Editors: Gregory Armstrong & Suzanne Lipsett
Cover photograph: "Rebirth," Shirley Hadley
Cover design: Marvenco
Drawings: Tom Soltesz
Typesetter: TBH Typecast, Inc.
Editorial Assistant: Nancy Carleton
Book production: Schuettge & Carleton

Manufactured in the United States of America

10   9   8   7   6   5   4   3   2   1

Acknowledgments

This book has been a great pleasure to write, in part because it engaged us in cooperative relationships with so many people.

First, hearty thanks to Peter Lindemann, whose friendship and influence have played a key role in the writing of this book. In long conversations, he clarified his own work and helped us to refine our understanding of biocircuitry; he also read our manuscript and offered many helpful suggestions.

We are grateful to many friends in England who have helped us over the phone and through the mails: Beryl Eeman, for her assistance in locating publications and photographs of her father; Pat Golby, of the Radionics Society; Michael Rust, of the British Society of Dowsers; Anne Atkinson; Jean Cormack (daughter of Aubrey Westlake); Bruce Copen; Mike Roberts; Leo Corte, of Delawarr Laboratories; T. Watson, M.D.; Annette Inglis; and Vicki Roberts, of *The Radionics Quarterly*.

In the United States, Michael Maffeo helped us again and again, beginning by providing us with our first copy of *Cooperative Healing*. Tom Brown, of Borderland Sciences Research Foundation, became our friend and resource, and it was Tom who introduced us to Peter Lindemann. During the earliest phase of our research, his predecessor, Riley Crabb (who kept Eeman's work alive in the United States for thirty years) gave us trans-Pacific research advice from New Zealand. We are grateful to those whose professional contributions helped us significantly: George Fritz, Ph.D.; Greg Neilsen; Thomas Hirsch; Kathleen Hirsch, C.A.; and Phil Thomas, who educated us about Edgar Cayce's work. Frank Aguirre; Richard Gerber, M.D.; Miki Shima, C.A.; Ray Himmel, C.A.; Steven Birch, of the New England School of Acupuncture; Steve Claydon; and Bob Nelson of Rex Research contributed time and energy to our research efforts, for which we are appreciative. Several personal friends, including Michael Setter, Richard Brown, Kathleen Lynch, James Steinberg, Tom Remus, David Rosen, Hal

ACKNOWLEDGMENTS

Okun, and Frank Marrero, freely gave us useful assistance, feedback, and support.

We are particularly grateful to Hal and Linda Kramer for their enthusiasm, professionalism and humor, and for bringing in Greg Armstrong and Suzanne Lipsett to edit this manuscript as only they could do.

We have saved for last our acknowledgment of our long-time spiritual teacher, Da Free John, to whom we are especially grateful. Da Free John first introduced us to biocircuits. Both personally and through his writings, he helped us understand the relationships between the "I" and the body, between the body and energy, and between energy and consciousness. With him we experienced these things directly in a way words cannot describe. Without that unique education, we would not have been able to write this book.

IMPORTANT

This book was not written by a medical doctor, and nothing herein should be construed as medical advice. *If you have a medical condition, please consult a physician.* None of the information or ideas contained here are a substitute for the advice of a licensed physician.

A Note About "Me"

Since this book is coauthored by two people, Leslie and Terry Patten, but written in the first-person singular, the question naturally arises: who speaks through its pages?

Let us describe our collaboration: Leslie began researching and writing this book in the fall of 1986. In mid-1987, Terry began writing the theoretical sections and polishing the text. Over the next year both of us lay in circuit many times, contacted various people for research purposes, rethought our ideas about biocircuits, talked, and reworked the manuscript again and again. We agreed, disagreed, and ultimately agreed. So this book is the work of a marriage partnership, utterly different from and greater than what either of us would have done without the other. It has been a large project; while doing it we have struggled and shared difficulties, surged ahead, and shared triumphs. Most of all, we have loved each other.

So who is the first-person singular? In some parts of the manuscript (for instance, in the chapter "Listening to the Unseen Body"), Terry's experiences are referenced in the first person. But from its beginnings, *Biocircuits* was written in Leslie's voice. Reading this book is something like listening to a couple tell a story: the first-person singular speaking through its pages is Leslie's, with her husband (like many husbands) sometimes interrupting.

June 1988
San Rafael, California

Contents

Introduction:
I *Am* Energy!

How I Came to Write This Book

I had read about it and heard about it, and I had even become convinced that it was of fundamental importance to human beings, but I had never been able to *feel* the "life force" in my body. Years after I had recognized the incompleteness of the scientific orthodoxy of my public school education and my Jewish upbringing, and even after years of studying Eastern religious texts, ancient and modern, and years of doing Hatha Yoga and sitting in daily meditation, I hadn't been able to break through. I couldn't feel a thing.

Even though doctors are not taught about life energy in medical schools in the United States, I knew that millions of people not only believed in its existence, but also claimed to *feel* this energy as it moved through their bodies. Many even claimed to be able to heal by contacting, harmonizing (resolving unharmonious patterns of energy), and strengthening this "life force." The healing art of acupuncture (which I was certain had validity) is based on this model of human life and health. I knew that life force had to be moving through my body or I wouldn't be alive.

Maybe I was just insensitive, or maybe all these reports about *feeling* the life force were largely delusionary. I didn't know for sure. But one way or another, this fascinating dimension of experience seemed unavailable to me.

Now, I was a somewhat unusual case: even though I was not a "sensitive" or a mystic, and even though I remained skeptical, even mistrusting, of the occult, I was stirred by a powerful religious intuition. So I read widely in Hindu, Buddhist, and Christian spiritual literature, and I sought out a spiritual teacher, eventually becoming a student of Da Free John.*

* *Da Free John, also known as Da Love-Ananda, is an American-born spiritual realizer, teacher, author, and scholar. Please see the bibliography for a listing of books by him that relate to the current discussion.*

Even so, I wasn't sure what it would be like to feel energy in my body; nor was I sure if I really wanted to. I was a little afraid of such a feeling. I wasn't even certain what there was that *could* be felt. I intuited the existence of a greater and higher force, or Consciousness, but I didn't see how that had anything to do with bodily sensitivity to the life force.

In the summer of 1976, I was invited to a small gathering at my teacher's house. This particular occasion was the setting for what he called a "consideration"—a remarkable and exhaustive exploration of a subject in spiritual terms—and tonight he was continuing his exploration of traditional and modern techniques for intensifying the life force. He had been talking about Kaya Kalpa, an ancient Ayurvedic practice reputed to produce remarkable rejuvenative effects under certain circumstances. He had also been discussing various unusual fasting practices, and even therapy that included the drinking of one's own urine! Such considerations were always lively and entertaining, but I was not sure how seriously they should be taken.

That night someone brought in an odd-looking pair of metal screens and handles with wires attached and described how a man named Eeman, working in the 1930s, had claimed that by lying in a certain configuration on these screens, the user felt energy moving in and around his body. Da Free John invited everyone to try out the screens and asked that people let him know if they felt anything interesting. The screens were set up in the middle of a room for the rest of the evening, laid out in the correct configuration (Figure I-1) for those who wished to experiment with them.

I forgot about this device until much later that night, when I walked through the room where they were set up. Since nobody was using them, I decided to lie down on them and try them out. If I felt anything at all that night, I forgot about it immediately.

Other people must have felt more than I did, because based

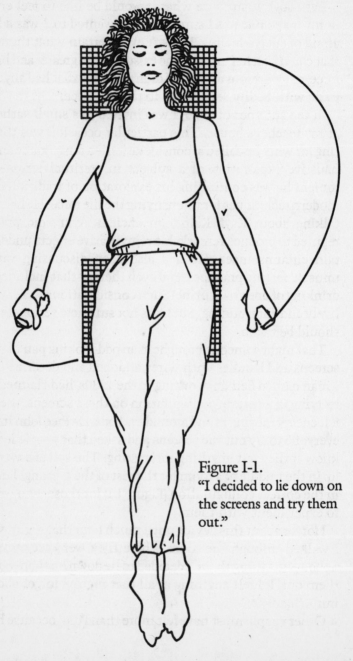

Figure I-1.
"I decided to lie down on the screens and try them out."

on the reports from others who had experimented with them as well as on his own experience, Da Free John began recommending these Eeman screens as an aid to balancing the body, particularly before meditation.

Several years later, one of Da Free John's students began to manufacture the screens for use by other students. By that time I had nearly forgotten my "nonexperience" with the screens that night in 1976, and I wasn't really interested in buying a set. Nevertheless, in 1980 my husband, Terry, brought home a set of these "Eeman screens." We played with them, and I began using them occasionally.

Gradually, over time, the miracle happened! I began to feel the life energy and to develop a growing sensitivity to the effects of the screens. As I became more sensitive, I began to use them more and more often. Eventually I was using them once or twice every day.

Not only did I notice subtle changes in how I felt while using the screens, but I also felt such changes throughout the day. As time passed, I became more and more sensitive to energy conditions. In turn, I discovered that I became saner, more balanced, and healthier by paying attention to the subtle flow of energy coursing through me. I could even strengthen my resistance to disease.

I found that the best time to use the screens was after work. At those times the results were especially pronounced. I had a stressful job, where I worked on my feet all day under fluorescent lights. The first thing I noticed while lying on the Eeman screens was my imbalanced energy. I felt throbbing or pulsing sensations, particularly in my chest or head.

Within minutes, energy began to move within and around my upper body. I felt this energy moving through and eliminating the throbbing sensations—which were, I learned, obstructions to the energy flowing freely—evening them out and creating a continuous, smooth, and intense flow of energy throughout my upper body. After twenty to thirty minutes, it was obvious that the experience was over. The energy in my body was harmonized and I felt nothing more from the circuit. Through the absence of sensation, the circuit let me know that the process had come to an end. After about ten minutes in circuit, I usually fell into a very deep and restful sleep. But I always awoke when it was time to quit and the screens had done their work. Afterwards, when I awoke, my natural reflex was to stretch and stretch and stretch. Never did stretching my arms and legs feel quite so good or so necessary as at those times.

After using the screens daily for several months, my experience began to change. Instead of falling into a deep sleep each time I lay in the circuit, I was able to stay awake while my energy began to "balance out." There was always a point, some time after the energy in my body began to move, when my breathing would release and become relaxed and full. Although I sensed that energy was moving inside my body, there was a stronger sense that this energy was also outside and around it, even pervading the whole environment. I was becoming sensitive to a larger, already existing field of life energy with which I was continuous. As my energy became harmonized with this greater field of energy, I felt a very pleasurable sensation of fullness in my chest that seemed to expand and engulf my entire upper body until I felt "lifted out" of my usual consciousness as a physical body. I was existing as a sphere of energy in and around my body. It felt as if no barrier existed between this sphere of energy, associated with my body, and a greater, more universal energy that surrounded me and seemed to extend everywhere. All was continuous, as if my skin had become transparent and permeable. Resting in this "energy body" was extremely pleasurable. Within it, my body, emotions, and thoughts seemed to come into harmony. After a minute or two, the sensation would subside and I'd return to a more ordinary state, once more identified with my physical body but feeling refreshed, energized, and relaxed.

Needless to say, this was a delightful, pleasurable experience. I began to use the screens more often. Although this experience of expanded energy didn't occur every time I used the screens, it happened frequently enough that I began to look upon these simple copper devices as a source not just of stress release but of intense enjoyment and pleasure.

I also liked to use the screens before meditation, as my teacher had suggested. Without them, up to a half hour of my meditation was sometimes occupied with watching my body trying to balance and harmonize itself before my attention was free enough to enter deeply into meditation. Using the screens virtually eliminated this waiting period.

The screens were also helpful for my health problems. For many years I had suffered various digestive disturbances, including allergy symptoms, liver congestion, and intestinal cramps. I used the Eeman screens when I felt particularly intense symptoms. *Every single time*, these symptoms lessened in intensity or completely disappeared. Unfortunately, the screens never eliminated these conditions permanently, but they did give me marked symptomatic relief.

All this was enough to convince me of the benefits of this simple device, and I became a regular user. When I first became aware of these effects, I had suspected that they might have been merely placebo effects, so I tested my experience many times. I would lie down without the screens at the time of day when I usually lay on them. Nothing would happen. Then I would lie in the circuit and, moving slightly, break the circuit midway through the process, carefully observing the effects. It was clear that the circuit provided a distinct, repeatable, beneficial effect, far beyond anything that could have been caused by simple resting. I was convinced of the legitimacy and value of the screens and deemed myself a satisfied customer.

But becoming a satisfied customer is a far cry from becoming an apostle. I didn't become convinced that this tool should be made known to large numbers of other people until a more dramatic experience occurred in the spring of 1986. This incident demonstrated to me that these screens were not just beneficial and useful, but were powerful, truly extraordinary tools for those interested in taking responsibility for their own health.

My husband and I were traveling through Burma. I was carrying a small pair of Eeman plates* to use for jet lag. I used them after each flight, greatly reducing and sometimes altogether eliminating my jet lag symptoms. I had been traveling for four months, and my sensitive digestive system had begun to react adversely to the foods I was eating in Asia. For a while I managed to minimize the symptoms by eating carefully, but in Burma I suddenly experienced a flare-up so severe I thought I'd have to leave the country. The choice of foods available was limited and the oil in particular bothered me. Each time I ate I became violently ill. Unfortunately, we had arrived in a very remote rural area, far from medical help or the possibility of quick departure.

The traditional Shan tribal-style dinner served at the hostel looked delicious, but I carefully avoided most of the dishes, eating only those foods I thought were "safe." But that night my symptoms worsened dramatically. I lay in bed unable to sleep. Violent cramps interfered with my breathing. My husband was debating whether to have me hospitalized in the nearest city. I wanted very much to stay in Burma, but unless this reaction abated quickly, we would have to leave as soon as we could.

I got out my Eeman plates and lay down on them while my husband touched my abdomen, using his hands to transfer

---

* *Eeman used copper mesh screens under the head and spine. Users have found that copper plates work just as effectively as the copper mesh screens, although the screens are more comfortable to lie on. A few people have reported that the plates are more effective for them than the screens. Others prefer screens, because they can be made larger than plates.*

energy to my distressed digestive system. At first, I began to feel the circulating energy only very faintly. Soon I started to perceive the pain and congestion as an obstruction in the overall flow of energy. Gradually, that obstruction began to loosen up and the healing energy began to flow through my liver and intestinal areas. After an hour I felt much better and began to enjoy the natural, balanced feeling of flowing energy I had come to associate with use of the Eeman screens.

We got up and took a walk. It was after midnight and the streets were very still. In the absence of streetlights, the stars crowded the sky brilliantly. We walked for more than an hour. Gradually, as I breathed deeply and walked, my strength and vitality surged. I felt *much* better. By the next morning I was well.

This experience convinced me: the Eeman relaxation circuit was a remarkable, extraordinary tool. I felt an urge to make this circuit known to other people. Someone, I felt, should write a book on the subject. The screens had helped me to experience and enjoy a new dimension of energy. Not only had my awareness and sensitivity been expanded through my experience with the Eeman device, but the screens had enabled me to achieve good health even under extreme circumstances.

I knew that if the screens could do this for me, then they could do the same for other people as well, even those who had no special training, talent, or experience. Upon our return from Asia, I began to research this device and all its related phenomena.

As we worked on this book, Terry and I tried each of the uses for biocircuits we discovered. At this point, we have lain in biocircuits innumerable times. We have gone further and further—and have noticed more and more.

Despite all I've learned, my most fundamental feeling about this inner exploration is that it has been tremendous *fun!* Certainly, this exploration has made me more sensitive, more aware, but this "new sensitivity" was actually just my ceasing to suppress something that was already innate. The real discovery and the real motivator has been the enjoyment. I *am* energy! And that is a great pleasure. I enjoy being balanced, I like to feel higher levels of subtle energy, and I love it when I'm radiant with unobstructed energy.

Finally, then, it is this enjoyment I want to share with you. Biocircuits have many important applications, an interesting history, and a whole science of their own. But above all, they are a source of balance, pleasure, and enjoyment.

What Is a Biocircuit?

Thousands of men and women have testified to the amazing and subtle efficacy of biocircuits over their sixty-year history. These simple, safe, nonmechanical implements enhance the flow of life energy by connecting different parts of the body with simple linkages of copper or silk. Biocircuits introduce no external electrical or magnetic energy to the body, and yet their effects seem nothing short of miraculous. Here are some of the widely reported effects of these simple devices:

- Users describe the primary and underlying benefit of the biocircuit as a consistent *balancing, relaxing, and energizing* of the whole person. Biocircuits are said to especially harmonize nervous system imbalances and to relieve *stress, fatigue, and enervation*.
- Biocircuits have been widely used with great success to relieve problems of *sleeplessness*.
- Biocircuits have also been used to promote *sensitivity to life energy* and to develop or enhance *psychic abilities*.
- Biocircuits have been used as a tool for facilitating *personal growth* by aiding in the work of contacting and releasing hidden emotions, memories, and patterns of bodily tension.
- Biocircuits have been used to magnify the deep psychological and bodily effects of *visualization* exercises, *affirmations*, and intentional *reprogramming*.
- Many biocircuit users have reported success in preventing, reducing, or speeding recovery from *exhaustion after airplane flights*.

Some users report that using biocircuits helps them prevent or speed up recovery from colds and flu. Others say that the devices mitigate or relieve allergic reactions. Still others claim that they help to ease back pain and speed recovery from muscular injuries.

There is no scientific basis for making any medical claims for these devices. Nonetheless, my own experience has led me to believe that biocircuits are profoundly effective in balancing life energy and promoting a deep and useful "intelligent trance" state. That other benefits may accrue as a by-product of energy balance and profound relaxation I have no doubt.

You may already have experienced the principles upon which biocircuits work. "Laying on of hands" is an example of a "natural" biocircuit, where the external conductive medium is another person's body. This healing art involves the communication and circulation of energy via the hands of the healer. Jinshin jyutsu and shiatsu practitioners use these biocircuit principles, frequently holding two points on clients' bodies to create a circuit, or flow of energy, through their bodies. Randolph Stone, the founder of polarity therapy, was the first contemporary body worker to state the biocircuit principle explicitly. He taught his students that the practitioner should use his or her body to create a bridge between areas where energy is overly concentrated and areas where energy needs to flow more strongly. That's exactly what a biocircuit does.

When I began this book, the only biocircuit I was aware of was L. E. Eeman's original "relaxation circuit," an example of which I saw at Da Free John's house that night in 1976. Later I discovered research that went beyond Eeman's to create new forms and uses for these circuits and introduced additional elements into the circuit to heighten the effects.

As I saw a new field of research unfolding, I realized a new term was necessary for describing it and all the different circuits emerging. I wanted a term that would encompass three basic criteria. All these circuits

1. are placed near or against the body at two or more points, connecting them to form a "circuit";

2. (a) enhance the movement of energy in the body and/or
   (b) actually conduct this energy;
3. conduct or enhance the movement of the body's own
   energy—*without* the introduction of external sources of
   energy, such as electricity, magnetism, heat, or light.

After considering many different words, I decided upon the term *biocircuit*, because it completely expresses the spirit of these devices. *Bios* is the Greek word for "life." The Greeks used it to refer to that intangible yet essential force that vitalizes all living things. As used in this book, the term *biocircuit* refers to a circuit powered *only* by the inherent life energy of the body.*

My research and personal experience have convinced me that biocircuits can be powerful and valuable tools for human health, well-being, and personal growth owing to these effects:

- **Biocircuits bridge imbalances in the body's energy system**, either by inducing deep relaxation and rejuvenation or energizing an otherwise enervated bodily condition. They do not directly increase the quantity of energy in the system, but instead release the body's energy flow in a way that makes it more available for well-being or the natural healing process.**

---

* Some readers may wonder why this book ignores Dr. Reinhard Voll's "Dermatron," Dr. Hiroshi Motoyama's "AMI Machine," the Mora device, and the Acupath instrument, along with TENS (Transcutaneous Electrical Nerve Stimulation) and other technologies that pass electrical currents through the body. These devices use an external source of electricity, and thus cannot be regarded as "true" biocircuits.

** The exception to this rule is a modified biocircuit that connects a true biocircuit with outside vibrational influences, such as substance circuits or cooperative circuits. If a true biocircuit is connected with an outside influence that introduces external energy (such as magnetism or electricity) into the circuit, it would not be a biocircuit as defined here.

- **Biocircuits frequently induce an intelligent trance of body and mind.** In this state, the usually distinct boundaries among the body, emotions, mind, and higher psychic functions become less pronounced and more transparent. A person in an intelligent trance can explore supernormal conscious experiences, perhaps explore and release deep, previously inaccessible material more easily than usual, and receive and absorb new, desirable programming at a deep level of the being.

- **Biocircuits appear to carry a great deal of information** relating to the physical body, emotions, mind, and even psyche of the individual. Biocircuits can be modified so that we may "tap in" and decipher this information or introduce other information directly into the body's energy field. This may prove to have important applications for diagnosticians or healers.

Mechanism, Vitalism, and the Science of Biocircuitry

The research and investigation described here stands on the "cutting edge" of our exploration of the human organism, human health, and dimensions of human awareness. Nonetheless, certain scientists would probably denounce it as anecdotal, subjective, unscientific, and vitalistic. I want to mention that attitude directly, at the beginning of our discussion.

In the West, the study of life energy is generally viewed in the tradition known as "vitalism." Vitalism asserts that the laws of physics and chemistry alone cannot fully explain the processes of life, but that life itself, *élan vital*, is at least in part self-determining rather than mechanistically determined. In other words, life itself is a conscious force, a mysterious principle, that operates in ways that are mechanistically inexplicable. Folk traditions and esoteric spiritual traditions universally describe vitalist views of human life and consciousness.

"Mechanism," on the other hand, sees the body entirely in terms of its physical and chemical processes. According to mechanism, belief in a life force is irrelevant to a complete understanding of biological processes.

In the first half of the twentieth century, at least as far as the most influential Western scientists were concerned, mechanism flatly won its debate with vitalism. Mechanist thinkers provided a fruitful foundation for scientific experimentation, which resulted in numerous important discoveries. Certain theories put forward by vitalists were disproven. On that basis, vitalist thinking was discredited, even though vitalism per se was never conclusively disproven. At that point, respectable biologists of the mid-twentieth century began to shy away from references to "life force." Proponents of such ideas were even denounced as superstitious and unscientific.

But recently Western attitudes have been undergoing a revolution. Many Westerners, including some influential biologists, are now convinced that living things are animated by intelligent, living energy. And a growing body of scientific discoveries suggest that life energy may be essential to an understanding of the human body-mind. These discoveries have seriously challenged the mechanistic view of living systems.[1]

As a result, investigations into life energy can no longer be viewed as irresponsible, even when such investigations do not seek to equate life energy with electricity, magnetism, or any other mechanical force. A new, more sophisticated vitalism seems to be emerging.

The Science of Participation

My experience and research have convinced me not only that a life force exists but that understanding its characteristic behavior is fundamental to the study of human bodies and human health.

The mechanistic methods of Western science can help us to complete our picture of our physical bodies, but they cannot see behind it. They cannot identify and explore the life energy that animates that mechanism. At most, scientific findings may imply that "something else," something not yet mechanistically explainable, is at work in living things. For real understanding of life energy to emerge, abstract scientific knowledge must yield to direct participation.

Biocircuitry offers a tool with which we can explore these dimensions of ourselves directly. With its help, we can use the ineffable connection between the physical body and the subtle energy that pervades it to expand our conscious experience. Using this technology, we can visit a realm that is intimate to us all, but that is still mysterious and only sketchily mapped. Biocircuits are an invitation to direct experience and a tool for exploration. But don't take anyone's word for this. Instead, try biocircuitry for yourself. Experience directly what the mind of mechanistic science can only doubt.

Notes

1. For an intelligent contemporary theoretical overview of vitalism that comprehensively discusses healing modalities addressing life energy directly, see *Vibrational Medicine*, by Richard Gerber, M.D. Gerber also provides useful summaries of a large number of experiments conducted by reputable scientists that lend credibility to the energy model of living processes used here.

Biocircuit Experiences: Stories From Users

In the following section, a wide range of biocircuit users describe their personal experiences. I contacted a random cross-section of biocircuit users; some wrote out their observations and others I interviewed. Before beginning the discussion of the historical and technical aspects of biocircuitry, I include these stories to illustrate the wide range of personal experiences others have had with biocircuits.

Executive Power-Napping

I started using biocircuits about two years ago, when I was in charge of a rapidly growing business. We were under extreme production pressure all the time, and my workday was full of stress. By midafternoon, I needed to refocus, so I had begun to take fifteen-minute breaks during which I put my feet up, closed my eyes, and relaxed.

I was given a copper biocircuit, and I tried using it during my midafternoon break. I passed out and woke up refreshed. I began using it regularly. Even when I didn't fall asleep, I could feel tension and stress running out of my body, and when I got up I was much more refreshed than I would have been just from a nap. There was a definite difference between the effects of the biocircuit and a regular nap.

I have used biocircuits regularly ever since—every afternoon at 2:30 or 3:00. When I'm most imbalanced I generally fall asleep; but when I'm relatively balanced I usually stay awake. Either way, I feel much better. I keep one pair at home and another in my office.

After I am done, I am not groggy. I stand up, stretch, take a couple of deep breaths, and feel refreshed and grounded. It is as though I have just had a deep, deep sleep, but in only

fifteen minutes. I resume work after using them feeling like I do when I arrive in the morning, and I have that kind of energy right through the end of the day.
—Jacques Drouin, President, Corporate Consulting Firm, San Francisco, California

Dramatic Energy and Tears of Joy

My first biocircuit experience was much more dramatic than I expected it to be.

As soon as I grasped the copper handles my hands began tingling slightly. Then, almost immediately and lasting for the first five to eight minutes, I had a heightened sense of the energy in my body. I could feel it moving everywhere, and I could even feel the pathways it was taking. The energy movements were uneven and jerky at first. It felt like the energy twitched and even jumped several times. The energy was not smooth or congruous at all.

Then my legs began to hurt. I felt a quality of obstructed energy in the lower part of my torso and in my legs. Then my body began to feel weighted down, as if gravity had become much more powerful, pulling me towards the floor. Then all of a sudden I felt my body surge. My body felt like it wanted to rise. I felt pulled up even while gravity continued to keep me down. The motion seeming to raise my body was stronger. This became an experience of intense joy. While in this exalted state, I could see a garden and smell the flowers in it. During this time I experienced so much joy tears came to my eyes. This experience was very real. After a few minutes the joy subsided.

Then my body felt as if it were tilting up at a forty-five degree angle from the floor. It was as if I were levitating. I got a little scared and tried to equalize my body. Then I became aware of the obstructed energy in my legs and lower body again. Then my right arm jerked involuntarily. Immediately, it was like

18

a dam had broken. The obstruction of the energy in my lower torso released. I could feel energy pulsating throughout my body. It was a wonderful feeling.

At that point I knew intuitively that I had finally accomplished what I had set out to accomplish (even though I hadn't known exactly what to expect before I began). I could still feel a flow of energy in my body, but it was perfectly even—it felt "meshed." In the beginning, the energy seemed to flow only in one direction. Now it flowed equally through my whole body in a balanced pattern, with both sides functioning as a whole. I knew I had finished "balancing my life energy" (which is what I had been told the biocircuit would do), and so I let go of the copper handles.

—Phoebe Ronsheim, Personnel Manager, New York City

Grounding and Integration

I am sensitive to many different energies: my own energies and the energies of others. I often find myself struggling to clarify whose feelings are going through me—are these my feelings or are they the feelings of someone else?

When I travel it is common for me to experience difficulty in reestablishing the foundation sense of becoming grounded again in the body. And it is exactly for these reasons that I became interested in the biocircuit.

I use the biocircuit when I first recognize the signs that I am becoming fragmented. The initial experience is both the intensification and the magnification of my symptoms. I lie on the biocircuit, relax as much as possible, and allow the body to go through its stages of change. This is not always easy to allow, but I persist because I know what's on the other side. After ten minutes or so I feel these energies begin to settle down. This occurs for a few minutes, and then, like magic, I feel a remarkable reintegration of myself. A deep sense of balance moves through me and I am refreshed and restored. I have been using the copper biocircuit for eight years and never leave home without it!

Recently I was introduced to the silk Lindemann circuit. My first use of it instilled in me a great sense of respect for it. I found it to be as penetrating and realigning of my energy as any acupuncture treatment that I've had.

—Kathleen Lynch, Larkspur, California

Enhanced Recovery

Note: This story is anecdotal only. There is no scientific basis for any medical claims made for biocircuits.

For the last eight years I've used the biocircuit for relaxation and regeneration, enjoying its balancing effects on my body's energies.

Naturally, I took the biocircuit to the hospital when I was to have major surgery. I was amazed at the profound effect it had on my recovery. Also, my doctor and members of the nursing staff commented on my speed of recovery.

My experience in using the biocircuit after surgery includes the following:

1. *Marked reduction in the need for pain killers.*
2. *Deep rest and relaxation, even though I had difficulty because of noise and nursing schedules.*
3. *Calming and clearing of my mind of the negative mind forms I experienced as my body released the anesthetic drugs.*
4. *Balancing of my emotions, so the experience of surgery was a positive one.*

I feel the biocircuit greatly enhanced my body's ability to heal itself.

—Leanne Reily, Dog Breeder, New Orleans

Extending the Effective Workday

I have noted a strong feeling of energy flowing through my body, sometimes quite intensely in certain parts. I feel greatly relaxed (less mentally scattered) for about six hours after only one-half hour in the relaxation circuit. I now make a regular practice of using this circuit when tired. It greatly extends the length of my effective working day.
—William Tiller, Professor of Material Sciences and Engineering, Stanford University, Stanford, California

"Similar to a Good Meditation"

In high school I injured my lower back playing contact sports. About seven years ago those injuries flared up very seriously, causing pain and discomfort when I walked, drove, or sat for any length of time. It was during this time that a friend made me aware of the Eeman biocircuit. I made a set of copper screens and began using them daily.

The screens helped to balance my energies and release a lot of tension and pain from my back. Using the screens helped to neutralize quite a bit of the pain during my healing crisis. It felt very similar to a good meditation, leaving me more balanced and relaxed after a twenty- to thirty-minute session.
—George Conley, Spiritual Counselor, Sausalito, California

An Engineer's Analysis

I have used the copper Eeman biocircuit for several years, primarily as a means of restoring calm and balance at the end of my workday. I find it extremely beneficial in energizing my body and reestablishing emotional and physical equanimity.

I usually spend ten to twenty minutes in the copper biocircuit. It seems literally to clear out the channels of energy in

21

my body, and I have no difficulty observing this process as it progresses. The process seems to focus initially in the vital region of my body, over the solar plexus. As the energy is freed and restored in this area, the balancing process very naturally and quickly acts on the rest of my body.

Recently, I experimented with the silk Lindemann circuit. I noticed a distinctly different process occurring. The silk circuit seems to act on my entire body at the same time. The process seems more subtle and less dynamic, and also appears to require a longer time to become effective. However, the silk medium produces a very deep and resonant calm that is very natural and peaceful.

—Brian O'Mahony, electrical engineer, San Rafael, California

These stories give us a glimpse of a wide range of experiences. Some people use biocircuits to reduce stress and extend their workday. Others use them to restore equanimity and balance bioenergy. Still others say they have used them to fortify physical well-being. Some use them to integrate the body-mind, others to promote deep sleep. Some people have seen biocircuits provoke blissful, almost mystical experiences. Some of the people we have quoted use biocircuits daily, while others use them only on specific occasions.

Interestingly, all of these people engaged in these explorations themselves. By using biocircuitry they were able to enjoy these benefits without the help of a therapist or instructor. Their stories point to an important aspect of this discussion: biocircuits are a *self-empowering* tool with a sixty-year history of verified efficacy.

I
Amazing New Tools

Chapter 1

Leon Ernest Eeman:
Pioneer of Biocircuitry

London 1915. War raged throughout Europe. A young pilot in the Royal Flying Corps prepared for takeoff. He checked his instruments, accelerated down the runway, and began the ascent. The plane was barely aloft when the fuel pipe blew off and the plane came crashing into the air force barracks. The plane was reduced to rubble, but the pilot, twenty-seven-year-old Leon Ernest Eeman, was still alive, although in serious condition. His left shoulder blade was crushed and he had a severe concussion.

After his recovery, Eeman went on to fly in Egypt, the Sudan, Greece, and France, until 1918, when he was admitted to the hospital again with an array of symptoms traceable to his 1915 crash. Between March 1918 and August 1919, Eeman spent time in five different hospitals. When he was released he was deemed "100 percent disabled, permanently unfit for any duty." Eeman later wrote,

After a few weeks in a hospital bed, two things became clear to me: first that I was in such pain and felt so ill that I couldn't live much longer, and second that if I was nevertheless to recover I should have to do the job myself, as none of the different physical treatments I had received had relieved either the acute head and spine pains and the unbearable insomnia caused by a head injury, or the exhaustion brought on by war flying in four different countries, with dysentery and malaria added for good measure. I concentrated all I had left in me on my wish to recover and to do so by my own means, in view of the failure of allopathic medicine. This wish became so powerful that one morning, weak though I was, I wildly struck

my bedside table with my fist and shouted at my orderly that
"Whatever anybody thought, I would get completely fit again,
even if it took me ten years." To this the orderly replied: "There
is one thing about you, sir, when you go down the sink, you'll
go down with a joke!" I will never forget those double-edged
words.[1]

The Relaxation Circuit

Eeman's plan for recovery slowly began to take shape. While
still in the hospital, he recalled Jesus's admonition in the New
Testament: "Heal the sick by the laying on of hands."

Why the particular emphasis on the hands? Eeman pondered.
Could hands radiate? And do we react to the radiations of our
own or other people's hands independently of suggestion? And
why "hands" and not "hand"? Eeman concluded that the plu-
ral suggested human beings were bipolar, rather than unipo-
lar, organisms.

Eeman had observed that children heal very quickly. He
believed that it was their abundant life energy that made this
possible. He also noted that the body does most of its repair
work during sleep, when it has all of its energy at its disposal.
Eeman reasoned that this healing energy was not gross muscular energy, but the subtle energy of the life force itself.

Were healers, then, people who possessed an abnormal quantity of this healing energy, which they could then transfer to
receptive subjects? Eeman speculated that it was actually the
contact between the healer and the patient that produced the
healing. In that contact, healer and patient complete a circuit
in which an exchange of healing energy occurs. Sick and old
people understand this circuit-healing effect instinctively.
When they are tired or ill, it is because they have run out of
energy. They instinctively lock hands and feet to recharge their
circuits. Once they have recovered enough energy, they separate their extremities and stretch. Healthy, growing children

sleep spread-eagled, but, in illness, they too close circuits. Old, sick, tired, and cold animals also link their extremities, separating them and stretching when they have overcome their energy shortage. Observing these phenomena, Eeman concluded "that when energy supply is low, living things unconsciously connect their opposite poles, much as one puts a horse-shoe magnet away with a keeper linking its two poles."[2] This intuitive recognition of the linking of opposite poles had enormous significance in Eeman's later work.

Eeman's conclusions can be summarized as follows: human beings radiate energy, and this energy radiates more powerfully or accumulates more readily at specific areas of the body. These locations can be linked together to create a circuit that enhances recuperative processes and produces a flow of energy. This energy is the energy of life. It alone is the power that heals. In addition, this energy can be transferred, or conducted, between individuals. This may occur naturally, as when lovers embrace, or intentionally, as when healers use their hands.

On the basis of these observations, Eeman created a closed circuit, using copper as his conductor. Eeman called his new device *the relaxation circuit*. By using wires to link the hands to the base and top of the spine, he produced the same results as those that occur when the hands and feet are instinctively linked—warmth, relaxation, and increased energy. He found that the recuperative flow of energy is greatly increased when the head and base of the spine, two of the body's major power centers, are accessed by the right and left hands (refer back to Figure I-1 in the introduction).

Within two years after his release from the hospital, Eeman had developed a series of techniques with his new circuit that had restored him to better health than he had ever known. He was now able to "command sound sleep at any time of the day or night."[3] For the drugs and narcotics he had been given for so many months, he substituted frequent long periods in the relaxation circuit (sometimes adding conscious relaxation techniques). The device not only speeded his recovery, but sensitized him to the life force, creating a circuit of energy flow that harmonized, balanced, relaxed, and restored him to natural equanimity.

Completely intrigued by the healing power of the simple apparatus he had made, which he felt was a remarkable discovery, he wanted to share his technique with other victims of insomnia. Immediately after his recovery, he started accepting patients. In 1922, Eeman set up his consulting and treatment rooms at 24 Baker Street in London. He continued working there until shortly before his death in 1958. It was during those first years that Eeman met his life-long assistant, Mary Cameron. The following story by Cameron, related to a patient in 1962, describes this meeting. It is a wonderful illustration of Eeman's intuitive and spontaneous approach to his work:

I had left the place where I lived as I could not remain there any longer. I did not know where to go or what to do. I had no money and no training. I was only eighteen, and was carrying all my worldly goods with me as I walked down the streets of London. Suddenly, a gentleman came down the steps of a house, smiled gently at me and we spoke. After a short time he told me he had been waiting for me and that I would work with him. I went inside and there I stayed, learnt from him, and we worked side by side.

Soon after opening his practice, Eeman came to feel that healing others wasn't enough and that he had to seek acknowledgment from the medical field for the validity of his relaxation circuit. And so he initiated a long series of experiments.

Eeman's steady and prolonged use of his device was beginning to increase his own energy and vitality dramatically. He wondered if he could wire himself into circuit with his weaker patients, thereby giving them additional healing energy. Once again, Eeman's knowledge of "laying on of hands" sparked a new idea. If energy could be transmitted to another via the hands, couldn't it be communicated even more directly by linking the life energies of the two people via this copper circuit? From this idea emerged more than thirty years of research into "cooperative healing." Initially, Eeman entered into circuit with his patients one at a time. As his research progressed, however, he used more often six but occasionally up to twenty individuals in circuit. These cooperative circuits revealed many of the mysterious properties of the living energy. Numerous unexpected phenomena occurred only in these cooperative circuits. In the cases of some phenomena, years of experimentation were necessary to unlock their significance.

In more than thirty-five years of practice, Eeman treated hundreds of patients with a wide variety of complaints. Many of these treatments, which included cooperative circuits, myognosis,* and suggestion techniques produced significant results, including many apparently miraculous recoveries. Eeman enabled his patients to get relief from nervous, mental, circulatory, respiratory, digestive, and eliminative disorders, including headaches, high blood pressure, rheumatism, lumbago, and sciatica, to mention a few.

Eeman's most consistent and dramatic results were with cases of acute insomnia, including ones of long standing, in which he obtained almost "magical" cures. Eeman claimed that through the use of certain simple techniques in conjunction with the relaxation circuit, insomnia could be completely eliminated. In his book *How Do You Sleep?*, published in 1936, he articulated his philosophy of sleep along with his techniques for curing insomnia.

Although Eeman tended to credit all his healing successes to the relaxation circuit itself, some of the credit goes to the man. A measure of his therapeutic success probably resulted from his own healing capacities. Here was a man who worked

* *Eeman's technique for acquiring access to and fully releasing unconscious tensions. See chapter 8 for a full discussion.*

with this circuit every day for more than thirty-five years! In the process, I believe, he acquired some unusual abilities. Over time, he seems to have developed a remarkable, almost yogic, ability to transmit living energy, especially via his cooperative circuits. Not only was he greatly sensitized to the life energy, but he learned to use it consciously.

How the Relaxation Circuit Works

All Eeman's earliest subjects reported experiencing feelings of muscular relaxation, warmth, well-being, and drowsiness while in the circuit. Through observation and testing, Eeman noted a variety of physiological benefits as well, such as the slowing and strengthening of the pulse rate, a lowering of blood pressure (if it was high), and a deepening of the breathing. He concluded that the circuit "fosters sleep, recovery from fatigue and disease, [and] capacity for work and health in general."[4]

It wasn't long, however, before Eeman noticed a pattern of atypical, sharply negative biocircuit effects. When the device was connected to the body in *reverse* configuration—the right hand connected to the head and the left hand to the base of the spine—people described adverse reactions: they couldn't lie in circuit for more than a few minutes without feeling tension, irritability, and restlessness. Sometimes this reaction was so intense that subjects might throw up their hands to break the circuit. Obviously, Eeman's first order of business was to find out which configurations produced relaxation and which produced tension, and to understand why.

Eeman began his investigation into these questions with an intuitive guess. Using an electrical model, he theorized that, like a magnet, the human body is characterized by polarities and that therefore all individuals must be charged positively and negatively at different places on the body. He speculated that this "human polarity" would contain an electrical potential, and that the life force (which Eeman called the *X force*) would then run continuously between these polarized terminals. Eeman felt that his relaxation circuit facilitated the flow of living energy between these differently charged terminals. He believed that by connecting areas of the body with dissimilar charges by means of a conductive medium, he could create a relaxation circuit. Conversely, connecting areas of similar charge would create a tension circuit.

Proceeding from this hypothesis, Eeman began a series of experiments on both humans and animals that spanned seven years. His aim was to map the positive and negative polarity patterns in the body and thus to gain control of his relaxation-circuit experiments.

For these polarity experiments, he used thin copper foil disks in place of copper gauze mats, because these one-inch disks could be connected anywhere on the body. In one experiment, he connected the left hand to the upper lip and the right hand to the chin. This experiment demonstrated to Eeman a vertical axis of polarity. If the left hand was connected to a place closer to the brain than the right hand, a relaxation circuit formed; otherwise a tension circuit was formed.

In 1925, after thousands of polarity tests, Eeman concluded that the human body demonstrated "electromagnetic opposition" along *three* main axes: vertically, or head to feet; horizontally, or right to left; and laterally, or back to front. As a convention, Eeman called the right hand positive and the left hand negative, the head positive, the spine negative, the back of the body positive, and the front negative. He found that the front-to-back axis was significantly weaker than either the head-to-foot axis or the right-to-left axis. He thus restricted his research to the latter—the two stronger axes (Figure 1-1).

These polarity experiments showed that the spinal line is a major conduit, and that both the hands and the feet are extremely strong terminals. For his circuit, Eeman decided to concentrate exclusively on the most primary and powerful energy terminals in the body. Intuitively, he had made use of

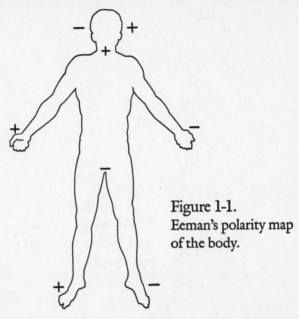

Figure 1-1.
Eeman's polarity map
of the body.

these very same powerful terminals since his experiments first began in 1919, but on the basis of these experiments he now developed a deeper understanding of the logic and hidden science behind his circuit. He learned why using copper for the screens and wire as a conductive medium, and linking the head to the left hand and spine to the right hand, with the feet crossed at the ankles, initiated a very strong relaxing and balancing effect. This circuit facilitated an unobstructed flow, causing the energy to move in something like a figure-eight pattern (Figure 1-2). (In a right-hander, the flow of energy is always from the left hand to the right hand.) When this pattern was reversed (i.e., the right hand was connected to the head [+ to +] and the spine to the left hand [− to −]), a tension circuit formed.

The only application for the tension circuit was to rebalance the body after it had been in the relaxation circuit too long. Eeman discovered this primary therapeutic application for the tension circuit after patients fell asleep in the relaxation circuit for extended periods. Upon awakening, some patients felt

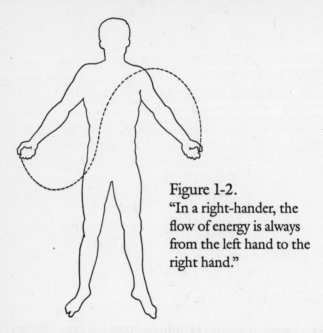

Figure 1-2.
"In a right-hander, the
flow of energy is always
from the left hand to the
right hand."

imbalanced and tired. This enervation was readily relieved
when they lay in the tension circuit for a short period. Eeman
observed that when a subject switched from the relaxation to
the tension circuit, there was a time lag before adverse reactions appeared. On the other hand, when the subject changed
from the tension circuit to the relaxation circuit, Eeman
observed signs of a subjective sensation of relief immediately,
"usually signaled by a sigh."

Occasionally, Eeman ran across a patient for whom a tension circuit formed a relaxation circuit. This occurred in only
about one percent of his patients over the course of his entire
practice. Eeman found that after only four half-hour treatments
in the tension circuit (their preferred circuit), spaced several
days apart, all of these patients with "reversed polarity" began
to prefer the normal relaxation circuit.

Eeman also experimented with simply flipping a switch that
would reverse the circuits while the patient lay unaware of the

---

Box 1-1

At a public demonstration of my cooperative group technique, I begin with a little theory about the relaxation and tension circuits and right- and left-handedness. I then ask four members of the audience to volunteer to rest on my four couches in the relaxation circuit. Amongst those who come forward, a tall man, no longer young, very gentle and dignified of bearing, introduces himself as a doctor. With charming courtesy, he assures me that although what I have explained is entirely contrary to all his experience, he is not only willing but anxious to put it to a practical test. I complete the relaxation circuit through my four subjects and for a quarter of an hour they rest in obvious peace. I then reverse the circuit unknown to them, when they all immediately display clear signs of restlessness and tension, and inside a minute the courtly gentleman violently throws away his handles and jumps off his couch, saying: "No, I can't stand that!"[5]

---

change. Eeman would note the patient's response. In every single instance, the patient quickly asked Eeman to stop whatever he had just done. He used this technique many times to wake patients out of deep sleep (see Box 1-1).

The relaxation circuit, on the other hand, had numerous benefits. In fact, Eeman spent his entire life discovering possible applications. Among his first discoveries were several general rules for using the circuit. First and foremost, the user *must completely relax* while in circuit. Without full relaxation, Eeman warned, the benefits of the circuit could be obscured or even reversed.

He also observed that the copper gauze mats did not need to be in direct contact with the skin. Clothes, blankets, and even cushions did not prevent the circuit from being formed.

The length of time one spent in the relaxation circuit was also important. Ten minutes seemed to be a minimum, but thirty minutes or more appeared to give better, more conclusive results. When treating specific illnesses, Eeman recommended a series of weekly treatments of up to one hour in duration with himself lying in circuit with the patient. Any enervation from too long a session in the relaxation circuit could be easily corrected by a few minutes in the tension circuit.

Eeman kept careful records of patients' descriptions of their experiences in circuit. He found that they followed a definite pattern. Initially, a wide variety of sensations might occur: intensified physical symptoms, emotional releases such as laughing or crying, exaggerated energy movements causing the body to twitch, or possibly no sensations at all.

Then, a distinctly new phase began. This was usually characterized by a deep sleep or at least very deep relaxation. Such an experience in the relaxation circuit had a definite end. The user would either spontaneously awaken or simply become aware when nothing more was going to happen. The awakening was frequently accompanied by a period of deep stretches and yawns. Eeman theorized that such stretches were a means of releasing the physical causes of unconscious tension (such as an excess of lactic acid in the muscles) and of expending some of the energy accumulated while in circuit. Not only did the circuit produce sleep, but for some reason the sleep produced in circuit was of a peculiar nature. Subjects constantly commented that the sleep they experienced in circuit was far superior to normal sleep, making them feel far more recuperated in much less time than usual.

"Sleep is work, and not mere rest; work of repair, recuperation, metabolism."[6] Eeman speculated that the relaxation circuit connected the body to the energies it needed for repair, and that these energies flowed abundantly enough to overcome muscular tension, nervous irritability, and mental anxiety. He felt that the process came to an end once the maximum charge of vital energy was reached and the functional needs of the body satisfied. At that time the user would awaken spontaneously.

Eeman's Early Professional Work

By the end of the 1920s, Eeman had published two books, *The Subconscious Made Conscious* and *Self and Superman*. He had also laid the groundwork for his next two decades of research.

The 1930s were a time of ripening and great unfolding in Eeman's work. It was during this time that Eeman did his foundation work for cooperative circuits and established many of the principles of biocircuitry. (For a full discussion of cooperative circuits, see chapter 12.)

Most importantly for Eeman's career, a network of vital research contacts began to form. His work came to the attention of leading English researchers in the new field of life-energy sciences. These included Oscar Brunler and Dr. W. Guyon Richards, both of whom endorsed Eeman's third book, *How Do You Sleep?*.

In 1935, Eeman began a correspondence with J. B. Rhine of Duke University, North Carolina, the leading scientific investigator at that time on extrasensory perception. This exchange resulted in Rhine's introducing Eeman to J. Cecil Maby, the well-known researcher in the area of dowsing. Rhine described Maby as a "brilliant experimenter, well able to assess what real worth there might be in [Eeman's] observations and afford instrumental demonstration and quantitative measurement of [the] facts."[7] Maby and Eeman eventually became closely associated. Within a few months of their introduction, Maby was doing tests on the Eeman circuit with such apparatus as cardiographs, pneumographs, psychogalvanic reflexometers, myographs, and other equipment. Maby carried out experiments for four years, and in these investigations verified that the phenomena Eeman observed did in fact occur, independently of suggestion. Maby writes in his introduction to *Cooperative Healing,*

So far as I have gone, it seems abundantly clear that Eeman is dealing mainly, if not always (since suggestion and psychiatric effects are practically impossible to eliminate entirely from a practice such as his, as he himself recognizes) with perfectly reflex physiological responses by his subjects to radiesthetic stimuli of some short-wave electro-magnetic kind. Such radio fields can be proved to exist physically and objectively, both as to emission and reception by living organisms, in relation to the nervous system in particular.[8]

Ten years after they first met, when Eeman was writing *Cooperative Healing,* Maby was still in the process of deciphering some of the more subtle phenomena that occurred in circuit.

It was during these years that Eeman, with Maby's help, completed his testing with various types of cooperative circuitry. Maby also assisted Eeman in testing the use of drugs and other substances in circuit and participated as a subject in many of the experiments.

The thirties saw Eeman complete extensive telepathic experiments and perfect his techniques for relaxation (myognosis) and conscious suggestion. Although originally conceived and described in his earlier books, these last two techniques were fully developed during this time.

Eeman's Optimal Circuit

In 1942, after more than twenty years of research using his basic circuit connecting the right hand to spine and left hand to head, Eeman discovered what he regarded to be a superior circuit. Instead of circulating this X force through the subject's central nervous system in a kind of S shape (see Figure 1-2), he connected the head and spine screens directly, placing the wire under the whole of the subject's spine. "This would bathe

the subject's spinal cord in the field of the X force which flowed between left and right hands"[9] (Figure 1-3). Eeman began "blind" testing with himself and his assistant, Mary Cameron, and proved the superiority of the new circuit.

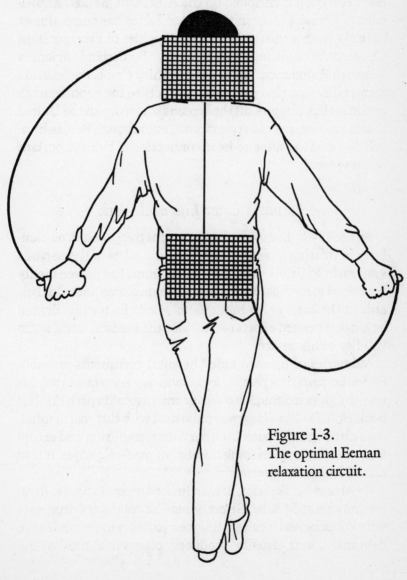

Figure 1-3.
The optimal Eeman relaxation circuit.

Eeman also conducted "blind" testing of his new circuit on many subjects, all of whom reported feeling a marked difference between the new and the old circuit and pronouncing the new one more effective. Interestingly, this "superior" circuit has never been mentioned on the American market. Knowledge of Eeman's work in the United States has come almost entirely from a thirty-eight-page pamphlet of excerpts from *Cooperative Healing* published by Borderland Sciences Research Foundation. Assembled by Riley Crabb, Borderland's former director, this pamphlet neglects to mention Eeman's optimal circuit. Thus, all the screens sold today in the United States use Eeman's old-style circuit, even though Eeman himself declared the spine-to-head connection to be an important improvement.

Eeman's Later Life and Work

By the 1940s, Eeman had a successful track record, particularly in treating insomnia and other disorders of the nervous system. In addition, the cooperative circuit had proven highly beneficial to fever patients. With these successes under his belt and on the basis of his meticulous scientific testing, Eeman began determined efforts to convince the medical world of the validity of his device.

Memories of his own failed hospital treatments probably fueled Eeman's new passion for convincing hospitals to test his new drugless techniques on fever and insomnia patients. His book *How Do You Sleep?* was published with this goal in mind. And although the book brought him recognition and acceptance among an increasing number of medical people, it also elicited great skepticism.

To silence his skeptics, Eeman invited many doctors to demonstrations at 24 Baker Street, where he conducted drug tests with cooperative circuits, using four patients in circuit. These demonstrations usually produced observable results and swayed many doctors, but generally his claims were countered with arguments that the findings were subjective, highly susceptible to suggestion, and may have involved telepathy.

Eeman's summary book, *Cooperative Healing*, was dedicated to "the research workers of London Hospitals." In it, he described most comprehensively his twenty-five years of research, still yearning for the acknowledgment by the medical profession that was never to come. Although *Cooperative Healing* was first published in 1947, Eeman wrote most of it during the war, perched in a London warden's post and composing chapters during lulls between air raids and on quiet nights.*

Even though the British medical establishment never accepted his new therapeutic tool, Eeman's work became increasingly popular among British health practitioners interested in the growing fields of radionics, radiesthesia, and homeopathy. These three life-energy healing "sciences" concern themselves with the unique vibrational frequencies associated with the life field of every living form. By reading or influencing these frequencies via the methods of these systems, practitioners in these fields attempt to liberate or enhance the body's natural healing process.

Probably through Maby's influence, Eeman became an early member of the British Society of Dowsers, where he frequently lectured. When the society formed its first council in 1946, he was a founding member. By 1953 he was elevated to vice president, a post he held until a year before his death in 1958.

Starting in the early 1940s, London saw exciting things begin to happen in the field of radionics. George and Marjorie de la Warr were developing new instruments and exploring new territory. Eeman participated in this revival by using radionic equipment to measure the effects generated by his circuit. Using three volunteers, one of whom was Marjorie de la Warr,

* *The complete edition of* Cooperative Healing *was out-of-print until 1987, when Health Research (Mokelumne Hill, California) reprinted the text.*

Eeman measured glandular rate changes before, during, and after use of the relaxation circuit. He also measured differences when drugs and homeopathic remedies were introduced. When the First Congress of Radionics and Radiesthesia was held in London in May 1950, Eeman was a speaker and committee member.

In 1947 Eeman met the prominent natural healer Aubrey Westlake, author of *The Pattern of Health*. Westlake was a medical doctor who, from 1938 until his death in 1985, conducted an energetic and comprehensive investigation of holistic health. He eventually became one of the most important spokesmen of the midtwentieth century for alternative approaches to health and healing. Besides contributing important insights to Eeman's work, Westlake helped legitimize that work through his own endorsement and by using the relaxation circuit with his own patients.

Westlake ranked Eeman's pioneering work in the field of life-energy research with that of Oscar Brunler and Wilhelm Reich. "[Eeman] has, to my mind, re-discovered and applied in a unique manner 'the laying on of hands.' . . . It is to be hoped that Eeman's work will not be overlooked or forgotten, as he has a very great contribution to make both in the physical and in the emotional and mental fields of therapeutics."[10]

Although many health practitioners used Eeman's relaxation circuit in their practice, Westlake became the first physician to use Eeman's technique of placing substances in circuit therapeutically.

Eeman's reputation grew among homeopaths as well. With Eeman's approval, Eric Powell, a prominent British homeopath, developed a device that allowed him to insert homeopathic formulas easily into an Eeman substance circuit. Eeman also began experiments with homeopathic remedies placed in circuit.

In 1954 Eeman gave a lecture under the auspices of the British Society of Dowsers entitled "Interim Report After Thirty-Five

Years of Research." It was to be his last professional publication.

In 1955 Eeman finally moved from the 24 Baker Street office to a larger house in London's outskirts where he planned to live and house his research practice. But before he was able to use it for his work, his health failed. Eeman came down with an illness whose diagnosis I have not been able to discover. He never recovered. Eeman died in 1958 after a fall, never having recovered from his prolonged illness. He was sixty-nine.

According to Westlake, considering Eeman's robust strength and general good health, Eeman's death "was probably due to the fact that he took too many of his patients' illnesses on himself" through his extensive use of cooperative circuits.[11]

Notes

For full source data, see the bibliography.
1. Eeman, "Interim Report After Thirty-Five Years of Research," p. 4.
2. Ibid., p. 9.
3. Eeman, *How Do You Sleep?*, p. 64.
4. Eeman, *Cooperative Healing*, p. 17. All references to this book are to the 1947 edition.
5. Ibid., p. 25.
6. Ibid., p. 183.
7. Ibid., p. 72.
8. Ibid., p. 5.
9. Ibid., p. 80.
10. Westlake, *1950 Speech Before the Radionic Congress*, p. 18.
11. Westlake, *The Pattern of Health*, p. 67.

Chapter 2

Silk Biocircuits and the Work of Peter Lindemann

It was Dr. Aubrey Westlake who first suggested the idea of a silk biocircuit to L. E. Eeman. In 1938 Westlake retired early from his first career as a general practitioner working in British hospitals to devote his complete attention to identifying exactly what was responsible for the healing process and determining how that process could be accelerated.

Westlake sought to understand *vis medicatrix naturae* ("the healing power of nature"), which had been the "golden fleece" of the healing arts since ancient times. What was the mysterious force that "did" the body's healing? Westlake investigated numerous disciplines—from Bach's vital force in flowers, to radionics, to Reich's orgone work—always asking, "Is the healing power in all these methods the same force?" Westlake's conclusion was, Yes! The force identified by the ancients was the same force operative in all these varied fields of healing.

When Westlake met Eeman in the late 1940s, he was intrigued and deeply impressed by the new science of biocircuitry. Westlake believed that the operative force in the Eeman circuit was this same ancient power, *vis medicatrix naturae*. Westlake suggested that a relaxation circuit be built of *silk* to test this idea. In making this suggestion, Westlake was drawing upon the research of two modern investigators into this force, Baron Karl von Reichenbach and Dr. Oscar Brunler.

In the early 1800s, Baron Karl von Reichenbach earned a fortune in iron, steel, and metallurgy. As an industrialist and chemist, he discovered creosote and paraffin. In 1839 he retired, devoting himself entirely to scientific research. Working mostly with the properties of light and magnetic fields and their subtle counterparts, he accumulated an abundance of experimental data on a mysterious force that he termed *Odyle* or *Od*. He proved to his satisfaction that Od was a force in its own right, one quite distinct from heat, electricity, or magnetism, and the same one acknowledged by the ancients. Reichenbach recognized that this force not only possessed polarity (he termed the right hand negative and the left hand positive), but that it could be conducted by metals, glass, resin, silk, and water.

Oscar Brunler, working in this century, used the term *biocosmic energy*. This was an energy that radiated from and pervaded everything. It too could be conducted. His work showed that all electrical nonconductors, such as mica, ceramic, and silk, were good conductors of this energy.

Westlake suggested to Eeman that he try substituting silk pads for the copper mesh mats and silk cords for the copper wires on his relaxation circuit. Both Reichenbach and Brunler claimed that silk was able to conduct this unknown force, Westlake pointed out. Were Eeman to obtain the same results with silk as with copper, he argued, this would prove that this force was *not* electrical, since silk does not conduct electricity.

Throughout his research, Eeman had suspected that he was working with a force similar but not identical to electromagnetism. In *Cooperative Healing*, he referred to this X force as "quasi electromagnetic," since it commonly evidenced powers beyond those of electromagnetism. For instance, he discovered that his circuit continued to work even when a wire was cut and placed on a glass surface. The glass conducted the energy flowing in circuit. But Eeman refused to follow up on this discovery, considering a thorough investigation of the true nature of this force beyond his competence. The phenomenon was so similar to electromagnetism, he argued, that he could continue to use its terminology with confidence. However, in 1949, after much prodding, Eeman agreed to make the silk test but decided to carry out a much more elaborate and conclusive test than Westlake had suggested.

First, Eeman and Cameron tested the circuit using silk only. The circuit worked! Then, as a further test, Eeman did a controlled experiment using drugs in a silk circuit. His six subjects showed the exact same reactions that they would have shown with copper. This convinced Eeman beyond a doubt that the X force was not electricity. In fact, Eeman later wrote, "Baron von Reichenbach demonstrated *that silk was a better conductor for the X force than copper . . ."* (italics added).[1] In *The Pattern of Health*, Westlake recounts how these tests "completely vindicated and endorsed my suggestion. Vis Medicatrix was not electrical, whatever else it might be."[2]

Unfortunately, the discovery of silk as a conductive medium came near the end of Eeman's life. In response to Westlake's idea, Eeman conducted the experiments through which he confirmed the fact that silk conducts the X force. Eeman even stated that silk was superior to copper as a conductive medium, but he did not live long enough to conduct significant experiments using silk. In fact, Eeman described his experience with silk only twice, once in his 1950 lecture to the British Congress of Radionics and Radiesthesia, and again in an obscure 1954 lecture, later published in the journal of the British Society of Dowsers. It would take another researcher, working in the tradition of Eeman and Westlake, to perfect and explore the silk biocircuit.

Peter Lindemann:
Contemporary Wizard of Biocircuitry

Remarkably enough, Eeman's biocircuit investigation and experimentation were almost universally neglected after his death. He left no students, and no apostles championed his invention or his research with it. The following three decades saw a great deal of related research into bioenergy: researchers mapped polarity, measured electromagnetic charges, and developed devices for intensifying, conducting, magnifying, balancing, and observing the body's energy field. For years, however, no serious researcher followed up on the pioneering biocircuit work of Leon Ernest Eeman.

When I began my research into Eeman's work, it seemed that it might still stand altogether alone. Nowhere else could I find a simple, external, nonelectrical device that helped conduct and circulate the body's own bioenergy. I found numerous individuals who were aware of Eeman's work, and those with direct experience universally corroborated its legitimacy: "Eeman's circuit works," they responded to my queries. "It's a remarkable and valuable tool." But as far as I knew, no one had extensively tested and extended his research.

Thus, I was delighted and intrigued when Tom Brown, director of Borderland Sciences Research Foundation (the publishers of the abbreviated version of Eeman's *Cooperative Healing*), suggested I contact Peter Lindemann, a researcher, Tom told me, who had been experimenting with Eeman's biocircuit for more than ten years! The little that Lindemann had published about his biocircuit research had appeared in the *Journal of Borderland Sciences*.

When I spoke to him over the phone, Peter Lindemann impressed me as a legitimate and knowledgeable researcher. I arranged to interview him at his Santa Barbara home shortly thereafter. It was an important meeting. I had already done extensive research into Eeman's life and work. To my surprise and delight, I found myself talking with the first significant biocircuit researcher since Eeman. His discoveries, for the most part still unpublished, helped define the field of biocircuitry.

Lindemann first discovered Eeman's screens while seeking a cure for his own "incurable" health problem, one that paralleled Eeman's own.[3] In Lindemann's case, it was a severe case of herpes simplex, with intense symptoms. In 1976, while living in Hawaii, he began using the screens regularly. "Herpes is stress related and the screens pulled a lot of stress out of my nervous system. I did show immediate changes using the screens. It just wasn't enough."

That led Lindemann to begin experimenting, looking for ways to maximize the benefits he received from lying in the Eeman circuit. He embarked on a long series of sophisticated experiments that eventually succeeded in rendering his herpes infection to the status of a "nonproblem."

In the process of healing himself, Lindemann became a sophisticated theorist about the principles underlying the biocircuit phenomenon. He also developed the first major advances in biocircuitry since Eeman's lifetime and became the most important contributor to biocircuit study since Eeman.*

Lindemann and Silk

In the late 1970s Lindemann worked at a clinic in Hawaii with a therapist who helped him build a biocircuit into a reclining chair. Lindemann also built a control panel that allowed him to create a variety of differently configured circuits at will and to wire other apparatuses into the biocircuit. The chair marked the beginning of an important dimension of Lindemann's experimentation.

Lindemann recounted how he ran tests with a great variety of materials, noting the different effects. "My first chair had aluminum screens," he told me. "This worked well until someone lay on it who was severely sensitive to aluminum. Within five minutes this person was climbing the walls. This told me that I had better begin experimenting with materials."

His experiments told Lindemann that every material in the biocircuit not only qualified the "feeling" of the energy in circuit, but communicated its influence directly to the energy

* The broad scope of Lindemann's work is described in greater detail in chapter 11.

field of the individual.* A small or minor element in the construction of a biocircuit, such as an aluminum rivet, could communicate powerful unwanted influences. Thus, he decided that it was extremely important to select materials for the circuit carefully. Lindemann explained:

Healing is a natural function of the body. Moving energy from one location of the body to another helps to release this self-healing process. If I place my hands like this [places right hand on the back of his spine, left hand behind his head], I can move this energy by using only my body. Of course, this is an uncomfortable position when maintained for too long. For that and other reasons, we've used external energy-conducting material to create this energy circuit. And once you start using materials other than your body, every material you introduce into that circuit qualifies the energy in some way. You have to be exceedingly careful, in fact, very strict to the point of precision as to what materials you choose to introduce into the circuit, because everything makes a difference!

This understanding later became a critical foundation for Lindemann's work with silk biocircuits.

In 1979 Lindemann read Westlake's book *The Pattern of Health*. Westlake's account of his experiments with Eeman intrigued Lindemann, providing a clue that opened up a major area of his own biocircuit research. Here was a new, nonmetallic medium for conducting the life energy. Nonetheless, Lindemann's work with silk didn't produce high-quality silk biocircuits until 1985.

When I started my experiments with silk it became clear that we were dealing with something very different from the

* This corroborated Eeman's extensive research with drugs in circuit and the subsequent work by the homeopath Eric Powell, the inventor of the autonormaliser. See chapter 5.

metals. First of all, the effect was noticeably "cleaner," subtler. When we got away from the metals, we started seeing much deeper and subtler effects using only silk.

Why silk works as a conductive medium is still mysterious, but the clue may be in the fibers. Wilhelm Reich suggested that all physical materials will demonstrate one of two fundamental responses to living energy to one degree or another: they will either reflect it or absorb it. Reich used this principle to build his orgone accumulator in 1940. He classified organic materials as absorptive and metals as reflective and found that reflective materials are *conductors* of orgone energy, while absorptive materials are *insulators*.

Silk, although organic, appears to function like a metal in its reflective ability. The silkworm secretes the silk fiber through a triangular opening. The silk is originally liquid, but dries as it emerges into the air. As it dries, it forms a single continuous smooth triangular fiber. The surfaces of the fibers are extremely reflective, as evidenced by silk's natural sheen. This reflectivity of the fibers may be the factor that explains why silk behaves in this respect like a metal. Says Lindemann,

I knew every material used in the copper circuit made a difference, and I found that every type of silk felt different in the circuit. Every color of material modified the energy. I set out to find the silk that felt most "neutral"—that is, a material that conducted the energy best and modified the energy least. In the end, it became clear that even what the silk worms had been fed was making a significant difference. After all this research had been done, I felt I had made a quantum leap.

Lindemann was the first researcher to systematically test a wide range of silk fibers. He spent several years finding the types of silk that conduct energy best. The type of silk, the color of the silk, and even the weave of the silk all made a difference. It was, of course, important that the silk be untreated and that no chemical dyes be used. As he refined the circuit more, Lindemann noticed that even the thread used to sew it together affected the experience in the circuit. He experimented with fibers, weaves, finishes, colors, and insulation materials. He also designed a variety of different silk biocircuits.

Lindemann did the foundation work through which high-quality silk biocircuits have been made possible. Westlake had suggested silk, and Eeman confirmed its value, but it has only been through Lindemann's work that silk biocircuits have been refined and made available even for limited experiments. In fact, the silk biocircuit reports in this book all describe experiences with prototype silk biocircuits designed by Lindemann.

Lindemann's Centrally Symmetrical Circuit

After years of using Eeman's basic relaxation circuit configuration, Lindemann felt he had reached the limit of its possibilities. He needed to improve the configuration if he was to derive additional benefits. He began experiments with alternative configurations:

I noticed that the energy running in the circuit was actually available at the ball of the foot. Crossing the legs as Eeman had people do, although it does allow a certain flow, is certainly not optimal. The real power points on the body are the base of the skull, the sacrum, the palm of the hand, and the ball of the foot. By placing the pads at those points directly, the effects are stronger.

Lindemann also wanted to find a "universal relaxation circuit," one that anyone could lie on regardless of his or her unique polarity. "The first universal relaxation circuit I found was a hand-to-hand, foot-to-foot connection, with the head and sacrum connected. This is an improvement of a circuit used by Powell, which connected the feet *only* by crossing the ankles."

Lindemann had studied the work of Eric Powell, the developer of the autonormaliser, a device for placing medicaments in the Eeman circuit. Powell used a configuration in which the head and sacrum are linked and the right and left hands are linked through his autonormaliser device.

Up until this time [Lindemann noted], Eeman, Powell and Westlake had always simply crossed the feet at the ankles. I decided to try a series of experiments where the ball of the foot was included. This necessitated the building of a three-circuit apparatus. I noticed immediately upon including the ball of the foot that the energy effect in the circuit seemed stronger.

I devised a switchboard that allowed me to experiment with all of the possible relaxation and tension circuits that can be created using the six major poles of the body [head, base of spine, two hands, and two feet]. I tried every combination. Very soon, I decided which one was my favorite. It was made by connecting the head to the sacrum and each hand to the opposite foot.

Like the first universal circuit, this circuit is "centrally symmetrical," identical on the right and left sides. Users do not need to account for their own polarity or for any differences between the right and left sides of their bodies.

I preferred this circuit over the hand-to-hand, foot-to-foot circuit because that circuit didn't create a flow up through the torso. It balanced the body left-to-right, but created no vertical flows as this one did. This "universal relaxation" circuit also created a different sense of balance than Eeman's original circuit. It seemed to include my whole body more than any of the other circuits. If you conceive of each part of the three-part circuit as creating a natural circular flow of energy through that area of the body, this circuit is unique, because each of its segments connects through the whole torso, even as it creates a strong flow left-to-right. I eventually called this my "core energy polarizer."

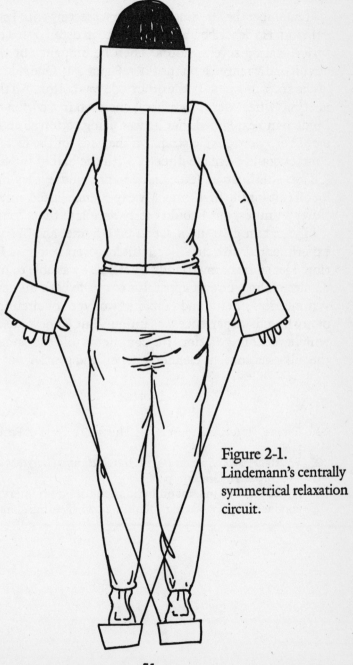

Figure 2-1.
Lindemann's centrally
symmetrical relaxation
circuit.

I remember the afternoon of my first meeting with Peter Lindemann. He described his work to me in detail over a conversation lasting several hours. Then he brought out the silk circuit and arranged it on the floor (Figure 2-1). One side of each of the six pads was silk, the other side was cotton. All the connecting "wires" were silk ribbon enclosed in a cotton casing. Lindemann explained that he was using cotton as an insulator. There were elastic straps on the pads for the feet so that contact could be made directly with the ball of the foot.

That afternoon at Peter Lindemann's house, I lay in a silk biocircuit for the first time. My experience lasted only about thirty minutes, but I could easily have lain there longer.

Lindemann gave me a set to take home, and Terry and I experimented with the silk circuit for several months. In addition, I let some of my friends try it out. I was able to use Lindemann's three-circuit apparatus to create both his centrally symmetrical circuit and Eeman's two types of circuits. Each of my friends' experience was unique. But whoever used it in whichever configuration, the comments told the same story: the silk was subtler, cleaner, crisper, and gentler.

Notes

1. Eeman, "Interim Report After Thirty-five Years of Research," p. 9.
2. Westlake, *1950 Speech Before the Radionic Congress* and *The Pattern of Health*, p. 68.
3. All quotes by Lindemann in this book are from interviews conducted by the authors. Reprinted with permission.

Chapter 3

The Alchemy of Copper and Silk

In theory, biocircuits can be built from a wide range of materials. To date, successful biocircuit technology has used either copper or silk, each of which possesses certain advantages. In general, copper seems to work on a grosser level of life energy, silk on a subtler level. Depending on the user's purposes, either effect may be desirable.

For everyday use, silk is my preferred conductive medium. Silk has several advantages over copper. Most prominently, I find silk to be a cleaner, more pleasing conductor than copper. Sometimes I feel an extremely subtle quality of irritation with the copper devices that I don't feel with silk. I also find the biocircuit effect crisper, sharper, and purer. Although with silk the biocircuit effect is subtle, it is also strong.

Nevertheless, when I need the biocircuit effect most, I sometimes choose copper, because of its more powerful, irresistible balancing effect. It also realigns the physical body with the relatively gross etheric energy most closely associated with physical processes. A stereo makes a good metaphor here: it is as if copper has a wonderfully strong "bass response," while silk offers an exquisite "high end." Because copper is easier to feel, I recommend it to most beginning biocircuit users.

Many people prefer the energy esthetics of silk over copper. Silk appears to harmonize obstructions at the level of feeling as well as those on the physical and energy levels. Some users say they feel it works on a heart level too, restoring not just vital energy but also open emotion. A small group of users feel almost nothing with copper, but respond very positively to silk.

Silk also allows for continuous, deepening relaxation. With silk, the biocircuit effect doesn't come to an end as it does with copper, so it is especially useful in facilitating the conscious

53

work necessary for personal and psychic development. Extended sessions allow ever-deepening psychic and emotional opening. Because it is subtler and because subtle changes form the basis for gross changes, the silk biocircuit experience can encompass more dimensions of the total body-mind. Perhaps this explains why some, although not the majority, of users feel a more powerful effect with silk than copper.

Nevertheless, copper has important applications. It circulates a grosser level of etheric energy strongly and works on a level more closely associated with the physical body and the body's electromagnetic field. Thus, it seems to be able to realign the etheric energies with the physical body in a unique way. Copper also seems to be more forceful in its reorganization of the body's energy-flow pattern. Silk is subtler; it does not override the body's energy-flow pattern. The best experience with the silk medium requires the individual's conscious cooperation with the biocircuit influence; copper asks less of the user. It is forceful and unmistakable in its effect. Thus, copper is effective even when an individual does not or cannot cooperate with its influence, which means that copper can accomplish things that silk cannot.

Copper offers a strong balancing influence and a boost of relatively gross life energy. This is helpful for those recovering from wounds or illnesses that have already taken hold. Copper is especially useful for people who are just becoming sensitive to feeling life energy circulating in their bodies. Someone who might notice nothing using the silk medium may readily sense the energy movement when using copper.

I found copper preferable to silk after I had a magnetic resonance imaging test, a medical procedure that required I be exposed to an extremely powerful electromagnet for an hour. This exposure distorted my electromagnetic field dramatically. I felt terribly agitated and imbalanced. I lay in a silk circuit for some time, but it lacked the power necessary to reharmonize my grossly imbalanced energy. Then I switched to a copper Eeman circuit. I stayed there for more than an hour and a half, the longest I had ever lain in a copper circuit without enervation. When I began, I was so imbalanced that the copper circuit mobilized a huge volume of etheric energy, producing an intense experience, akin to a meditative bliss state. Not only was the copper biocircuit experience intensely pleasurable (when the silk had been too weak to help me), but it restored my energy balance and sense of well-being.

In summary, I recommend copper biocircuits for stress release and deep relaxation to beginning users, to those who wish to become sensitive to life energies, for repolarizing the physical body to its relatively gross etheric and electromagnetic energies, and for stress release when especially imbalanced. Silk biocircuits I recommend for stress release and deep relaxation to those who are already highly sensitive to subtle energies, to those who wish to explore more subtle dimensions of sensitivity and experience, to those who desire a more esthetically refined energy experience, and to those who wish to empower other practices such as self-hypnosis, meditation, visualizations, brain machines, subliminal audio tapes, out-of-body experiences, and so on.

Irritation Versus Stimulation: What Is It We Feel in Circuit?

Peter Lindemann sees the differences between silk and copper primarily in terms of the relative purity of the two materials: "With the metals the effects of the energy in circuit are more noticeable, but I think it's partially because they have a subtly irritating effect on the system. A lot of what a person notices is this irritation, rather than the energy moving purely. Many people are not sensitive enough to know the difference between irritation and stimulation." Lindemann is talking about an extremely subtle level of irritation here. The primary effect of copper biocircuits is benign and stress reducing rather than irritating, as Lindemann himself is quick to point out. But as one becomes more sensitive, his suggestion makes sense.

Lindemann thinks that the biocircuit produces the sensation of the movement of the life force partly because it throws in a reference point. The movement of the energy through the body is now felt *in reference to* its movement through the copper or silk. Because silk is a subtler medium than copper, it is a subtler reference point and offers less resistance to the energy flow. Thus, the coarser the reference point, the stronger might be the sensation felt during the session.

Lindemann considers the totally unobstructed flow of life force to be inherently asymptomatic, because it is transparent. Since nobody's life energy is ever 100 percent harmonious, we all experience some imbalance—overconcentration and deficiency of energy in different parts of our total body-mind—most of the time. These imbalances function as obstructions to the natural flow of energy, sometimes producing symptoms as they provide resistance to the body's natural flow of energy. When we lie in a biocircuit, the flow begins to be restored. Where resistance was preventing the flow, now the life force *moves through* the resistance. What we feel while lying in the biocircuit is a symptom of the resistance, which qualifies or colors the energy. Our sense that "something is happening" is a perception of the movement of the life force, but it is related to our previous imbalance and obstruction.

I have noticed, and others have corroborated this observation, that I feel the least tangible evidence that "something is happening" when I am lying in the biocircuit in my most balanced and healthy state. The actual benefits in terms of balance and well-being, however, may be just as great or greater. The energy is flowing imperceptibly, but without obstruction, so it is harmonizing and deepening the living energy of my body-mind on subtler levels.

This observation raises an interesting point. Some people feel nothing when they first lie on a biocircuit. Is this because

56

they happen to have little or no obstruction to the flow of the life force? Perhaps, but probably not. In most cases, such people are just not yet sensitive enough to feel their obstructions. I have observed that people frequently need to develop a basic sensitivity to the life force (as I did myself). Once this develops, the "symptoms" of energy flow, or of obstruction to its flow, are easily felt.

Silk: The Perfect Wave

Peter Lindemann prefers silk because it allows deeper, more extended participation in the biocircuit effect than the copper permits.

Lindemann, like Eeman, noticed that the flow of energy in the biocircuit surged and subsided again and again before it eventually ended entirely. Eeman theorized that the circuit released energy in "waves, steps, or packets." Subjects linked in circuit together reacted spontaneously and simultaneously to these "waves" of released energy "as if controlled jointly by a single influence, external to themselves and yet clearly acting within themselves."[1] Eeman noted that this "wave" phenomenon would draw everyone first in the direction of relaxation and sleep and later toward "muscular contraction and awakening."

"With the silk," Lindemann comments, "you get a sequential rise and fall of the effect, but it just never stops. There are periods of greater and lesser intensity that seem to move in cycles, but I've never yet gotten to a place with the silk where the effect ended completely."

The reason for this difference, Lindemann believes, is that with copper the body itself simply indicates that it has had enough of the irritation copper causes, in spite of the relaxation effects, and stops the flow of energy, while with silk the irritation is negligible and the body never finds it necessary to shut down the flow. Lindemann feels that this idea explains the subjective sensation that the biocircuit effect "comes to an end" in the copper circuit and not in the silk circuit. In his opinion, "the body is both the source of the energy and a resistance to its flow. The biocircuit promotes the flow of energy, and that works to lower the body's internal resistance. When the body's internal resistance drops below the resistance offered by the copper, the circuit is effectively broken, and the effect comes to an end." It takes much longer for this to happen with silk—longer, in fact, than the period anyone reporting has spent in circuit. "This is my hypothesis, but other people who have used the silk circuits that I have supplied them all agree that the effect doesn't end." For another user's experiences with copper and silk, see Box 3-1.

A Psychic Views the Biocircuit Phenomenon

I wondered how someone who could "see" the energy moving would view the differences between the two biocircuit media. I was especially interested in what a clairvoyant might have to say about the subtle esthetics of the silk experience versus the gross power of the copper. I located an individual who has "second sight" and arranged an experiment.

Thomas Hirsch, who was born in Budapest, Hungary, is endowed with exceptional psychic sensitivity. After years of work, on his own and with a teacher, he developed these abilities to an unusual degree. For the past five years he has been working as a healer with his wife Kathleen in San Rafael, California. Kathleen, a certified acupuncturist and healer, feels for energy imbalances through the pulses and harmonizes them by inserting needles in points along the energy meridians. Thomas consults with her as he observes the movement and progressive changes of the person's energy field during treatment.

I asked Thomas if he would observe Terry and me as we lay in circuit, noting how our life energy changed. First, I lay in

Box 3-1
One User's Experiences with Copper and Silk

I have been a spiritual practitioner and a student of consciousness processes for about twenty years. I have paid special attention to the energy conductivity practices associated with certain yogas. I have used copper biocircuits to promote the relaxation and equanimity necessary to make use of real meditation. I have found biocircuits to be among the most useful simple tools at my disposal to help with the process of deep relaxation.

It became obvious to me through my study of the human body-mind and its higher processes subtler than the physical that copper biocircuits align the physical body to a greater etheric energy surrounding the body. They help release the knots, kinks, and disturbances of energy that tend to gather in daily living. In a relatively short time, and usually without fail, they accomplish this balancing function. Thus, biocircuits are among the most useful energy tools I know. When I use them I always experience a deep and profound pleasurable relaxation of my whole body-mind.

Recently I have used silk biocircuits. I find the silk far more subtle than the copper, which is gross in comparison. I find the silk to be more transparent. The silk does not add as much of its own quality to the biocircuit experience as the copper does.

—Hal Okun, Melbourne, Australia

an optimal Eeman circuit of copper. Thomas observed and described whatever changes he noticed in my energy body before, during, and after the session. Then Terry lay in a Lindemann silk circuit, while Thomas repeated the same procedures.

With *both* the copper and silk media, Thomas noticed three distinct phases. The first phase lasted anywhere from five to eight minutes and was characterized by an intensification of the imbalances in our energy field. The energy was in chaotic swirls, without any pattern of uniformity.

The second phase began around ten minutes after the sessions began. This was typified by a kind of polarization effect. Thomas saw the energy begin to collect at both ends of the body in vortexes around the head and feet. On either side of a midpoint near the waist, the energy polarized toward the ends of the body. Thomas described "standing waves" or waves of energy that measured six or more feet in height from the reclining body.

In the third and final phase Thomas noted a dramatic power surge. The intense disturbance of the body's energies gradually disappeared. The body appeared to be resting on a calm surface such as a still body of water. Thomas described this state as a respite from all the outside electromagnetic interferences, which perhaps explains the good feeling of this third phase.

There were distinct differences between copper and silk. With the copper, Thomas described the energy as "greenish-blue" and the effect as distinctly more mechanical and defined. The silk medium, he believed, was drawing on a higher or subtler level of energy. Its color was bluish-white. The switch into the second phase wasn't simply a "mechanical" polarization of the energies, but carried with it a feeling of lightness and heat. Thomas mentioned several times that the energy in the silk flowed more gracefully, as though it were more conscious, less mechanical, and more feelingly in touch with its own quality of movement. The power shift into the third phase was much stronger with silk than with the copper medium. Thomas also noticed that the shift took place at a higher vibratory-energy level. Thomas felt that the silk medium was definitely engaging a subtler energy, while the copper conducted a more mechanical or grosser energy. This corroborated my own observation that copper is superior for gross mechanical obstructions, while silk is the choice for conscious work, general balance, relaxation, and the enhancement of a person's feeling energy.

Jack Schwarz, N.D., has also compared copper and silk biocircuits. For the past thirty years, he has been known as a distinguished authority on human energy systems and voluntary control of ordinarily involuntary biological functions. His own paranormal abilities have been studied at the Menninger Foundation, Langley-Porter Neuropsychiatric Institute, and Stanford Research Institute. In general, his observations agree with those of Thomas Hirsch. Schwarz observed that copper biocircuits conduct a more readily visible, coarser level of energy than silk, and that therefore their balancing effect is easier to notice and feel—it is apparently "stronger." The silk effect, however, because it is subtler, can ultimately be greater than that of the copper.

Thomas had a few general comments about the biocircuit. He observed that it enhances sexual differentiation—that is, within it users relax more deeply into their natural sexual character and become even more distinctly male or female in their energy. Also, the circuit harmonizes the body energy but doesn't introduce any *new* energy into the system.* He understood how biocircuits would be very useful for people suffering from disturbances of the nervous system, such as insomnia, irritability, and nervous tension.

Thomas's observations served to reinforce what I and others had experienced, although I did, and still do, experience differences between the two biocircuits that Thomas did not see. Though Thomas described the visible energy in the two circuits as moving in almost identical ways, the different configurations of the circuit produce distinct experiences for me.

---

* *This comment applies to a simple circuit only. We didn't experiment with substances in circuits or cooperative circuits, and Thomas considered it possible that with a cooperative circuit participants would get the effect of additional energy.*

Still, Thomas's observations proved acute and insightful. He offered an additional confirmation of the effectiveness of the biocircuit and some useful and interesting suggestions about how both the silk and copper biocircuits may operate at the level of visible life energy.

Notes

1. Eeman, *Cooperative Healing*, p. 184.

Chapter 4

How to Select or Build and Use a Biocircuit

We recommend the following biocircuit configurations among all those tested over the last sixty years:

1. Lindemann's centrally symmetrical circuit
2. The "optimal" Eeman relaxation circuit
3. The original "general" Eeman relaxation circuit

The Lindemann Circuit

The Lindemann circuit is a powerful whole-body circuit. It circulates and balances life energy throughout the entire body both vertically and left to right. It can be either an energizing or a relaxing circuit, since it works toward balance in whatever way your body needs. I find that it powerfully promotes the intelligent trance state useful for deep work and visualizations.

Since this is a "universal relaxation circuit," the set-up will be the same for everyone, regardless of the individual's unique polarity. As shown in Figure 4-1, there are three parts to this circuit. The first part connects the base of the spine to the base of the head. The other two parts connect the hand to the opposite foot—the left hand to the right foot, and the right hand to the left foot. A strap or band holds the pad around the ball of the foot for direct contact.

I use this circuit most often with silk pads. For practical reasons, the soft silk is easier to place than copper screens or plates in direct contact with the bottoms of the feet. But this circuit works well with copper too.

The Lindemann circuit is energizing, calming, and harmonizing at the same time. The connections to the feet make

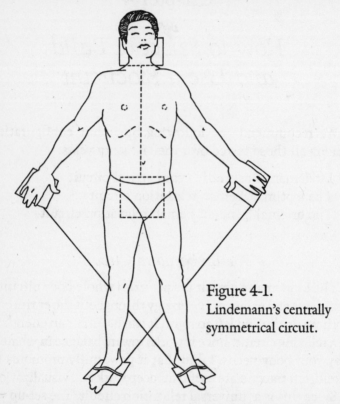

Figure 4-1.
Lindemann's centrally
symmetrical circuit.

it unique among the three major biocircuits. They give this circuit a grounding effect and help it to be felt throughout the whole body. A typical experience in this circuit is a sensation of being energized and aligned vertically along the spinal column all the way down to the feet.

The Optimal Eeman Relaxation Circuit

The optimal Eeman relaxation circuit is *the* circuit to use if you want to fall asleep! Eeman's final, streamlined circuit connects the base of the spine to the head, with the right hand connected to the base of the spine and the left hand connected to the head (Figure 4-2). The legs must be crossed at the ankles.

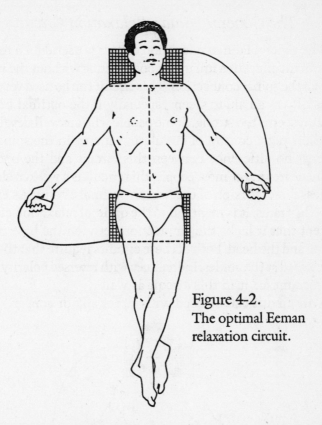

Figure 4-2.
The optimal Eeman
relaxation circuit.

If you have reversed polarity, a tension circuit will form when you lie in this circuit and you will need to reverse the handles.

This circuit deeply relaxes the chest and strongly circulates the life energy in the upper body. The head-to-spine connection provides faster and more powerful results than Eeman's original relaxation circuit.

The optimal Eeman circuit is effective with either the silk or copper medium. I generally prefer silk, but I use copper if I need a powerful boost of vital energy, if I want to balance my system from extreme agitation and intensely disturbed energy imbalances, or if I want to fight off physical illnesses that have progressed to the point of overwhelming physical symptoms.

The General Eeman Relaxation Circuit

The general Eeman relaxation circuit is useful for a milder biocircuit effect or a full upper-body feeling without the intensity of the spinal connection. This circuit can be used very successfully as an aid to sleep, especially if the optimal Eeman circuit seems too strong. Some people who are well-developed in their yogic control of circulating energy in the spine feel almost no difference between this circuit and the optimal Eeman circuit. For most people, this circuit is a weaker, slower, or less direct version of the Eeman optimal circuit. As Figure 4-3 illustrates, it is identical to the optimal relaxation circuit except that it lacks the connection between the base of the spine and the head. Both of these circuits require that the legs be crossed at the ankles. Individuals with reversed polarity need to account for it in this circuit as well.

This circuit can be used with either silk or copper.

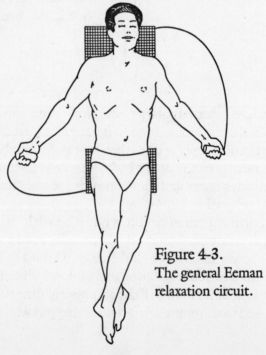

Figure 4-3.
The general Eeman
relaxation circuit.

Keys to Biocircuit Use

1. Relax completely. The key to optimal and effective biocircuit use is the relaxation of the voluntary muscles. The more
deeply you can relax, the more deeply you will be able to enter
into the biocircuit experience. There is no need for you to "do"
anything other than let go and surrender. The circuit itself will
help you to relax, but you must participate to achieve full
relaxation.

Use the biocircuit where you can lie down comfortably—
on the floor or on a bed, using pillows or under a blanket. It
is important that you relax completely, freeing yourself from
distractions or interruptions. Account for traffic noise, telephone calls, children, and housemates. Earplugs can be useful.

2. Feel your body. We tend to forget the body while the mind
races through its catalog of things to do, past events, and future
possibilities. Don't worry about your thoughts; thinking is not
a problem. Simply bring your attention to your body. Notice
how it feels. Watch for changes. If there are any sensations, such
as tingling and imbalances, simply bring your attention to them
and allow them. There is no need to change these feelings or
sensations. Only notice them.

3. Suspend expectations. Beginning meditators frequently
obstruct their growth in meditation by constantly judging and
interpreting their experiences. They frequently think that they
are more advanced than they really are, or that they are failing, that "nothing" is happening. Neither is true. With the
biocircuit, it is the same. Allow your experience to unfold naturally, and you won't get in the way of it.

4. Notice subtleties. Whatever your level of sensitivity, your
experience with the biocircuit will probably be subtle, perhaps
extremely subtle at first. Let that subtlety instruct you. Pay
attention to feelings you are used to ignoring. Your experience
may begin undramatically. That's fine. Be sensitive to all of it.
In time, you'll notice more and more.

5. <u>Allow up to thirty minutes.</u> Allow fifteen to thirty minutes for each biocircuit session. It takes a minimum of ten to twenty minutes to rebalance the body. Occasionally, especially with copper, more than thirty minutes can overrelax the system, producing enervation, although at other times as long as an hour can be desirable. *If you do become enervated, a few minutes in a tension circuit will correct this imbalance* (see appendix II).

Your time in circuit will probably be characterized by "waves" or "packets of energy." The energy experience will heighten, then subside, and then heighten again. Each wave will work at a deeper level. With the copper medium, most users report that the wave effect eventually ends, and when it does there is no further effect. With the silk medium, the waves continue virtually without end, and you must decide when you have had enough.

6. <u>You can participate consciously.</u> By itself, the biocircuit effect will relax you deeply and relieve stress. But you can enjoy more powerful results if you participate consciously in the experience. For instance, the biocircuit itself will not eliminate mechanical bodily tensions such as agitation caused by drinking alcohol or caffeine or sometimes associated with eating the "wrong" foods. The biocircuit effect *will*, however, create a state of deep receptivity that empowers visualization or affirmation exercises. By using that opportunity consciously, you can further calm the body, producing a deeper state of relaxation than would have been possible using the biocircuit only passively.

Principles to Remember

1. The bioeffect can take place through your clothes. It is not necessary for the biocircuit to make direct contact with your skin. Since the biocircuit operates at the level of the "energy body," the pads or screens can be positioned even several inches away from your skin. The biocircuit circulates life force that *pervades* and *surrounds* your body. With silk, I sometimes put the pads next to my skin in order to intensify the biocircuit effect, even though it is not necessary. Do not wear shoes when using a Lindemann circuit.

2. *Some people have reversed polarity.* After many thousands of sessions with his circuit, Eeman found that about one percent of the individuals he treated had reversed polarity—that is, their left hands and heads had the same charge, and their right hands and lower bodies had the same charge. *When they lay in the biocircuit, a tension circuit instead of a relaxation circuit formed.** People with reversed polarity should simply switch handles from one hand to the other, connecting the right hand to the head and the left hand to the base of the spine. Consider the possibility of reversed polarity only when using Eeman's two circuits. This condition is of no consequence when you use Lindemann's "centrally symmetrical" circuit.

Note: Left-handers usually do not have reversed polarity. If you are left-handed, there is no need to alter either of the two Eeman circuits (or the Lindemann circuit) on this account. Most left-handed people have opposite polarity *throughout* their bodies. Their polarity charges are the complete inverse (as with a photographic negative) of those of right-handers. Thus, lying in the usual Eeman relaxation circuit will still create a relaxation circuit. (Lefties *do* have to account for their left-handedness when lying in cooperative circuits with right-handers, however.)**

---

* *Oddly enough, Eeman noted, many of these people were being treated for disorders of the endocrine system. He also wrote that after four one-half hour treatments in their preferred circuit, most of these individuals' polarity returned to normal.*

** *See chapter 12 for a fuller discussion of left-handedness in circuit and cooperative circuits.*

Applications

Here are some examples of when people like to use biocircuits:

- *Before bed*. I prefer to use one of the two Eeman circuits when I want to get to sleep. As I doze off, I move the biocircuit out from under me; otherwise, I usually awaken just enough shortly afterward to move it. I prefer to do this so that I don't sleep on it all night.
- *After work*. Fifteen to thirty minutes in the biocircuit after work usually rejuvenates and energizes users for their evening activities.
- *Catnapping*. Biocircuits can provide deep refreshment in record time. We have heard many reports of businesspeople who use copper biocircuits for catnapping, which helps them maximize their productivity by recharging their systems in midafternoon. Whether they fall asleep or not, they emerge refreshed.
- *After flying*. After your flight, lie in circuit a few times that same day or once the same day and once the following day. I find this quickly restores and harmonizes my energy. People also sometimes rebalance themselves in circuit after spending long hours driving in a car.
- *Subtle body sensitivity*. The biocircuit will help familiarize and sensitize you to your etheric or subtle body. This is especially useful for people who meditate or do subtle body work, including massage and healing work, but it is enjoyable and helpful for everyone.
- *Inner exploration*. The biocircuit can be used as a booster for conscious personal growth work of many kinds. It intensifies visualization exercises, imagery work, and affirmations, and it also helps with the

70

absorption of subliminal messages. Biocircuits can ease access to deep emotional information in personal growth work.

- *Other occasions.* People frequently use biocircuits as preparation for meditation or yoga, as a way of fending off illnesses, as a way of coping with allergic reactions, and as preparation for demanding physical exercise, such as a competitive run or bicycle race. You will know for yourself when you want to lie in the biocircuit once you have become sensitive to the powerful effects of this energy tool.

Using Biocircuits for Stress Reduction

Biocircuits dramatically accelerate the body's natural release of psychophysical stress. Ideally, their use should be incorporated in a comprehensive program of balanced living. Biocircuits are not a panacea for stress. We cannot ignore the contributions of diet, exercise, sleep habits, and human relationships to stress and stress reduction. Nonetheless, actual levels of psychophysical stress can be lowered rapidly by means of biocircuitry, which makes it a powerful aid.

Biocircuits can be used in several complementary ways as a stress-reduction tool:

1. During the day, as a way of drawing off stress and deeply relaxing or catnapping
2. At the end of the workday, as a way of deeply relaxing and releasing the psychophysical stress associated with work activities
3. Before bed, as a way of inducing sleep
4. Upon arising in the morning, as a way of calming and centering before entering into the day's activities

Note that when people use biocircuits they frequently report unusually deep sleep at night, even if they did not use the biocircuit immediately before retiring for the night.

71

Tension and stress can be associated with a broad spectrum of factors, including caffeine, alcohol, rich foods, drugs, allergic reactions, and pain from physical injuries. Biocircuits do not magically eliminate these very real chemical or physical influences, and on occasion these influences may even interfere with the biocircuit effect. More commonly, though, lying in the biocircuit will help you become more sensitive to the automatic patterns of tension in your body.

For instance, I have lain in circuit while my body was zinging with hyped energy from too much caffeine. I relaxed as deeply as I could under the circumstances, and the biocircuit effect took place. I sank into the intelligent trance, motionless, deep, and conscious. But still the stimulant buzzed through my system. I was on one level very relaxed and on another highly stimulated. I did a visualization exercise, in which I visualized my heartbeat and nervous system relaxing, gradually slowing down. I visualized the caffeine draining out of my system rapidly, and my system coming into balance. Gradually, and only after I persisted in this visualization, it actually counteracted the effects of the caffeine.

Sometimes, when a person is exhausted, running only on nervous energy, the use of the biocircuit provokes a crash. The individual will sleep for ten to fourteen hours in a single night, conking out into a deep slumber "like a log."

I prefer to manage stress on an ongoing basis, using the biocircuit regularly to heighten my sensitivity, help me become integrated, and release the superficial stress associated with the day's activities.

Technical Tips

- *Posture.* The illustrations in this book show people lying flat in the circuit with their arms and legs straight, fully extended. This is not required. You can lie in circuit on a reclining armchair or even in an upright armchair with a headrest. You can lie on your back with your knees raised and bent. In the Eeman circuits, which call for your feet to be crossed at the ankles, you can improvise, bending the knees and bowing them outwards or placing the heels next to each other and touching your feet together by crossing them. It is only important that you be able to relax comfortably and completely.

- *Clearing the circuit.* Your bioenergy leaves its subtle imprint on biocircuits. This residue should be cleared periodically. I know three effective methods for clearing biocircuits:

  For silk. Throw the silk biocircuit into the drier for ten to fifteen minutes, set to *air fluff. Don't use heat,* because this can ruin the silk fibers.

  For silk and copper. Lay out the biocircuit in the sunshine for half an hour on each side. (Make sure your silk biocircuit does not get wet.)

  For copper. Place your copper biocircuit under cold running water for a few minutes.

- *Loaning your biocircuit.* Since the biocircuit picks up your energy and becomes attuned to your body, I recommend against loaning it out. If you do loan it out, clear it before you use it again.

- *Washing silk biocircuits.* Follow the washing instructions for silk carefully. The fibers can easily be damaged.

  1. *Never* use heat on silk, as it damages the fibers. Wash in lukewarm water. Either air dry out of direct sunlight or air fluff in the drier. Use a *cool* iron.

  2. Treat silk as you would treat hair; it is made of protein. Natural shampoos make a good soap. But remember to rinse it out thoroughly. You don't want any of those products to remain in your circuit.

Buying or Constructing Your Biocircuit

Remember when buying or constructing your biocircuit that every material makes a difference in the biocircuit experience. Metals other than copper can be used for the "copper" device as long as they are not toxic (as are lead, aluminum, or mercury). The character of a metal may determine its utility in a circuit. For instance, copper is a homeopathic remedy for collapse. Other metals that seem safe when used in biocircuit construction include carbon, stainless steel, bronze (a combination of copper and tin), brass (a combination of copper and zinc), tin, and iron. Some types of bronze, brass, and steel may contain traces of aluminum, so be careful. It is important not to use materials such as lead solder or aluminum rivets.

In building a silk biocircuit, be aware that the type of silk you use affects the quality of the experience in the circuit. Relevant factors include the weave, color, and finish; you may wish to experiment with different kinds of silk to see which you like best.

Since every color used makes a difference, unless a specific effect is desired, the fabrics should be white or natural (theoretically, your fabric could also include *every* color). We recommend that you wash all cloth materials *before* building your silk biocircuit.

Hardware List and Instructions

Copper Optimal Eeman Relaxation Circuit

- Two square or rectangular pieces of copper screen from 4- to 12-inches square (copper plates can be substituted).
- Three 4-foot strands of insulated copper wire.
- Two 4-inch lengths of 1-inch or ¾-inch copper pipe.
- Silver solder (also called jeweler's solder).

- Two #6 screw size ring-tongue crimp connectors to match the wire gauge you've chosen. Get tin-plated copper connectors. For an all-copper set, the plating can be filed off. These are used to attach the wire inside the handles.
- Two ⅛-inch length, ⅛-inch grip range pop rivets. Get copper rivets (frequently tin plated also) for an all copper set or steel for maximum strength. Again, these anchor the wire inside the handles.
- Cotton ribbon to sew around the outside of the copper screen.

Use the pop rivets and crimp connectors for connecting the wires to the handles. Lead-free soldering can be substituted for the rivets and crimp connectors, although it is not as sturdy. Then braid the wire into the screen and sew the cotton ribbon over it (around the outside of the screen for comfort). Alternatively, the wire can be silver soldered to the screen or bolted with small screws (not included in list). If copper screens are difficult to obtain, substitute bronze. Refer to Figure 4-2 to see where to attach the wires and the screens.

This device can be used to form the Eeman optimal relaxation circuit only. If you want to be able to form all three circuits with your copper apparatus, we recommend constructing a three-part apparatus, modeled after the Lindemann silk circuit described below.

Lindemann Silk Circuit

- Six pieces of white 100 percent cotton flannel approximately 6-inches square.
- Six pieces of white, high quality 100 percent silk approximately 6-inches square.
- 12 feet of 100 percent white cotton bias, wide enough to encase the silk ribbon, cut into three 4-foot lengths.

- 12 feet of ½-inch white 100 percent silk ribbon, cut into three 4-foot lengths.
- Two ¾ × 6-inch 100 percent white cotton strips.
- 100 percent white cotton thread.

Use the cotton bias to encase (insulate) three 4-foot lengths of silk ribbon. These are your three "wires." Each of the three wires has a pad attached at each end. The pads can be sewn, one side flannel, one side silk, inside out and then turned. Place the cotton bias with the silk ribbon inside the pad. Make sure the end of the silk ribbon is exposed so it makes good contact with the silk of the pad. This makes the circuit complete. Then sew the bias to the pad. The ¾-inch cotton strips should be sewn over the foot pads to hold them over the ball of the foot (see Figure 4-1). These can be sewn to the pad either before turning or after.

This is a basic construction plan for a Lindemann silk circuit. With this three-circuit apparatus, you can arrange all three major biocircuit configurations. For the optimal Eeman relaxation circuit, just overlap the pads of the third segment over one pad of each of the other two segments.

II
Health, Magic, and Pleasure

Chapter 5

Substances in Circuit for Energy and Health

Drugs, herbs, or other substances can be placed in biocircuits to influence the body's energy field directly. Eeman discovered this principle, and other researchers developed and refined its applications, leading up to Lindemann's most sophisticated work.* In the future, these principles may prove to have important applications for healers and medical practitioners. But even now, simple substance circuits can be used easily and effectively at home with a copper biocircuit.

Eeman's Drug Experiments

Eeman's early work with cooperative circuits uncovered a host of unexpected phenomena. By the end of 1927, in light of a growing body of test results, Eeman concluded that if one member of a cooperative circuit displayed an "abnormal physical factor," the other members in circuit *reacted in a similar manner.*

A drunk person in a cooperative circuit made the other members of the circuit feel slightly drunk. Members in a cooperative circuit with a menopausal woman could feel her hot flashes both coming and going. A healthy subject in circuit with a fever patient helped the patient's fever drop, and the healthy subject could sense a temperature change in his own body. When a cooperative circuit linked someone who had recently recovered from an illness with someone still suffering from the same

* *See chapter 11, which discusses Peter Lindemann's advanced work. See particularly the sections headed "The Circuit Carries Information," "Vibrational Grafting," and "Talking With DNA."*

illness along with perfectly well subjects, the sick patient's temperature fell even lower—just as if the convalescent patient were acting as a serum. This inspired Eeman to inoculate himself against a disease and then place himself in circuit with a patient suffering the same disease. This technique brought the condition into stasis.

These data suggested that the circuit could communicate influences via its own flow of energy. Eeman theorized that a subject in circuit radiated the equivalent of a "carrier" wave. When this wave was influenced by an "abnormal factor" originating within the subject's body, the entire circuit took on that abnormal frequency. The other members of the same circuit would then be affected.

Eeman speculated that any agent—whether it originated inside or outside a person's body—placed in a circuit would influence a circuit's members with its frequency. To test this theory, Eeman tried something new. He knew from repeated experience that when he placed himself in circuit with a fever patient her temperature would fall to a certain point but that it would drop no further no matter how long he remained in circuit with her. Within a few minutes the patient's temperature would drop from 103.5° to 102°, the "no-reaction" level. But instead of going into circuit with her, this time Eeman cut the copper wire and placed both ends in a glass of aspirin dissolved in water. Within minutes, the fever patient's temperature dropped to 100°! This experiment was the first evidence that the effect of drugs or other agents placed in the relaxation circuit was similar to their effect when taken orally.

When Eeman met Dr. Cecil Maby in 1936, they discussed controlled drug experiments. Maby's experience with scientific procedures and instruments would be invaluable in conducting such tests. But because of Maby's involvement in other projects, it wasn't until 1940 that their first documented drug experiments took place.

The first set of tests on "abnormal physical factors" took place on the weekend of April 26, 1940, at Maby's home in Bourton-on-the-Hill. Eeman and Maby devised an electrified chair wired with a relaxation circuit and a mechanism for inserting substances into the circuit. The chair was electrified because Maby insisted that a mild electric current be introduced into the circuit. He felt this would tend to "boost up" the reactions. Although Eeman argued that his own bodily "radiations" would provide a sufficient "carrier wave," and that even low-voltage electricity might be strong enough to mask the reactions of the drug, he finally agreed to Maby's electrified design, with the understanding that nonelectrified experiments would follow.

Eeman was the subject for these first experiments. Each unidentified drug was placed in the circuit, and Eeman described his reactions to it in detail. In every case, his descriptions matched the nature of the medicine administered, just as if that drug had been ingested orally! Excited by these results, Maby and Eeman decided to meet again soon and repeat the experiments without electrification.

The intensification of World War II delayed their meeting for some time, but this postponement proved a blessing in disguise. During the interim, a young pharmacologist visited Eeman and became fascinated with his work. Eeman placed him in circuit with ten different drugs in succession without giving any hint as to their identity. Each drug remained in the circuit for two minutes, during which time the pharmacologist described his sensations. After each drug, Eeman showed him the label, asking, "Is that what you would have expected from this drug?" In the first nine cases he replied, "Exactly," and Eeman was thrilled.

But when the last drug was placed in circuit, Eeman was very disappointed. The man's description of his symptoms was totally different from what he expected. The drug was caffeine and the young man experienced only peacefulness. When Eeman showed him the drug label and said, "Well, that's not what you would have expected from *this* drug," the pharmacologist became very excited and replied that it was exactly! He said he had a "caffeine tolerance" and experienced a sedative effect from the drug. For the pharmacologist, this test was the most convincing, as the results were diametrically opposed to Eeman's expectations, ruling out any influence due to experimental suggestion.[1]

The pharmacologist arranged to send a wider selection of drugs to Eeman. Shortly thereafter, a parcel arrived containing twenty-eight different bottles labeled A to Z, alpha and beta. The pharmacologist helped Eeman design an experimental procedure in which each drug was tested by both Eeman and Mary Cameron, and sometimes by Maby. The drug was to remain in circuit for at least two minutes, and up to five minutes if the subject did not object. (See Figure 5-1.) All the drugs were unknown to Eeman and Cameron. Only the pharmacologist knew their identity. He had even included some drugs with which he was unfamiliar in order to avoid telepathic suggestion!

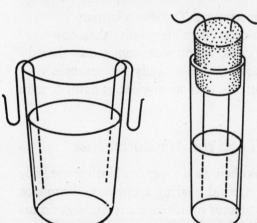

Figure 5-1.
Eeman's improvised method for introducing drugs into the relaxation circuit. The drug would be dissolved or diluted in water and the two probes would be connected to the wires leading to the copper pads.

Over a period of weeks, seventy-one "blind" tests were conducted on Eeman, Cameron, and Maby. Both the responses of the person in circuit and an observer's comments were recorded. These were compiled and sent to the pharmacologist. Only after the tests had been completed did he inform

Eeman what drugs had been used and how closely the subject's responses corresponded to their known properties.

Amazingly, the responses of the subjects corresponded very closely, and often exactly, with the known effects of the drug when orally ingested. The few inaccuracies appeared to be accounted for by the explanation that certain tests were administered too soon after other tests, and reactions to different drugs were therefore blurred. Some drugs produced pronounced and lingering subjective effects. Mary Cameron especially was disturbed for several days after the tests, and Eeman and Maby agreed that the drugs' effects were very potent even though they were not ingested.

Eeman concluded that drugs administered in circuit showed the same effects as oral doses with these differences:

1. Reactions were all obtained inside of two minutes— much more rapidly than if the drug had been taken orally.
2. The reactions were stronger. The doses Eeman administered to subjects were all smaller than one-tenth of one adult dose, which were sometimes shared by four or more subjects, and for only two minutes via conduction. The effects were as marked as a full dose to one patient.

Eric Powell and the Autonormaliser

The implication was obvious: if drugs could affect the body via the circuit, then natural healing agents could produce benefits too. The first doctor to use Eeman's findings on his patients was Aubrey Westlake, but the most substantial innovator was the homeopath Eric Powell. It was Powell who designed the autonormaliser, a device that simplified use of the substance circuit.

Powell, a homeopath and radionics practitioner, used the Eeman circuit in his private practice for years, regularly employing the optimal circuit on his patients to effect relaxation. He found the circuit especially useful for those suffering insomnia, abdominal distress, indigestion, general debility, and mental conditions characterized by excitement, restlessness, and moodiness.

When Powell learned about Eeman's experiments with drugs, he conducted his own experiments. His results corroborated Eeman's claim that medicines affected the body more quickly when placed in circuit than when ingested. Powell attributed this effect to purity: in the circuit nothing can contaminate the substance. Orally ingested medicines may go through chemical changes and contamination before being absorbed by the body.

Homeopathic medicines are especially vulnerable to contamination or antidoting in the mouth. Powell theorized that placing remedies in the relaxation circuit would eliminate this problem. The medicine could then enter the body directly as a vibrational energy; no digestion or assimilation would be necessary.

Homeopathic treatment is based on the use of extremely minute quantities of substances that in larger doses produce the same effects the remedy is intended to treat. Extremely minute remedies *cure* those same symptoms; the two principles of homeopathy are "like cures like" and "less is more."

Powell devised the autonormaliser to make it easier to insert remedies into the circuit. Bruce Copen, a noted researcher and innovator in the homeopathic and radionic healing fields, later improved the device. Powell and Copen used the autonormaliser in their private practices with great success for many years and also manufactured and sold the device to the public. Although he no longer sells the device, Bruce Copen still praises the effectiveness and success of both the Eeman circuit and the autonormaliser highly.

One advantage of the autonormaliser was convenience. The apparatus consisted of a simple circuit attached to a box that held the substance in a removable container. To Eeman's simple substance circuit, Powell simply added a ground wire to tap the earth's energy and provide additional healing force. Powell also modified the configuration. As Figure 5-2 illustrates, the head and spine are connected, while the hands are connected to the apparatus. All three wires, the earth wire included, run inside the box to a container filled with pure water plus the medicine.

Powell used his autonormaliser primarily with two medicines: a "medicament" he specifically designed for universal use, and the individual's own urine. He also occasionally used cell salts and other homeopathic remedies.

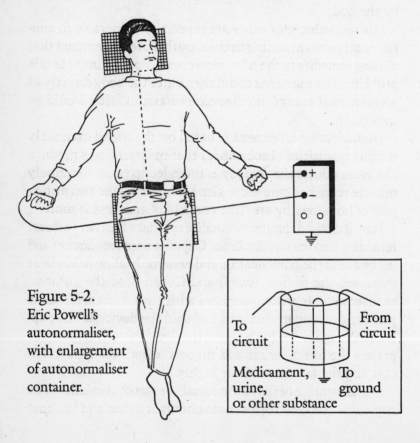

Figure 5-2.
Eric Powell's
autonormaliser,
with enlargement
of autonormaliser
container.

To
circuit

From
circuit

Medicament,
urine,
or other substance

To
ground

Powell's medicament was a homeopathic formula. As an original homeopathic theorist,* Powell formulated a natural agent containing all the mineral ingredients for his autonormaliser that would be of maximum universal healing benefit to any user. This substance "provided the system with a flow of the most vital and essential energies needed to encourage every organic process in the body, paying very special attention to the blood."[2]

Powell's other autonormaliser "medicine" was urine. Although it sounds bizarre to modern Westerners, the history of urine as a medicine dates back to antiquity. Folk medicine traditions beginning with those of the ancient Greeks and including those of the American Indians and of gypsies all over the world, describe the healing value of drinking one's own urine. Vedic texts describe the practice of *amaroli*, in which urine is taken as a yogic elixir.

Urine contains various hormones, minerals, and vitamins and numerous enzymes passed by the body that, when taken internally, are said to act as a tonic. Some people claim urine has cured a wide variety of disorders, such as heart ailments, kidney problems, colds, menstrual irregularities, and fevers. Its effectiveness is sometimes explained in terms of homeopathic principles: urine is a direct reflection of the body, containing minute traces of whatever toxins are associated with the body's disorders and weaknesses. When urine is taken internally, these same substances act homeopathically, alleviating the disorder. Thus it is claimed that urine is the body's own homeopathic remedy.

Most people find the idea of drinking urine repugnant, so it is not a popular home remedy. Powell felt he had answered this objection by placing the urine in the biocircuit. Using urine in the autonormaliser could charge the body with its healing signals as the tonic influences of the urine flowed

* *Eric Powell's book* The Natural Home Physician, *considered a classic in its field, is still in print and widely read.*

through the circuit. Powell felt this method produced results superior to those of the actual ingestion of urine.

Lindemann's Color Experiments

With their experiments with medicines, Eeman and Powell established a fundamental principle: the relaxation circuit effectively communicates vibrational influences into the body's energy field. In fact, the biocircuit is an especially pure and uncontaminated medium for transmitting such influences. Of course, this is true only if the biocircuit itself is uncontaminated—a biocircuit built of toxic metals such as lead or aluminum will communicate those vibrations into the biofield as well. This fact was implicit in Eeman's work but not explicit in his writings. It wasn't until years after Eeman and Powell worked together that Peter Lindemann understood and articulated the importance of pure materials and began his experiments with silk. These principles are fundamental to his advanced work with "vibrational grafting."

Even before he tried new materials, Lindemann made an important discovery: substances placed in the circuit not only influenced the body, but also registered in consciousness directly.

Lindemann's very earliest original experiments with biocircuits involved color. "I simply took two plates of copper, put a theater gel of the desired color between them, and placed that in the circuit. The color that I found most deeply relaxing, balancing, and de-stressing for my system was magenta. So I built a system where I could have magenta infused in the circuit while I shone magenta light on my body at the same time. This de-stressed me considerably and started making the herpes outbreaks further and further apart."

During the period in which Lindemann was doing his color experimentation, he was collaborating extensively with another researcher, Marty Martin:

86

In the system I built, the flip of a switch introduced a new color into the circuit. A green vibration, for example, could be infused into the energy of the circuit. After I put this system together I had Marty Martin lie in the circuit. I told him, "Okay, I can sense that each one of these colors has a different feel to it in the circuit. Let's see if you can feel the difference." I flipped switches he couldn't see, and thereby I tested whether he could identify by their "feel" the colors I introduced.

Well, Marty identified every single color. He never made a single mistake in telling me exactly which color I had just put into the circuit. I even flipped two switches, a red and a violet and he'd say, "magenta." That's what it was! Right after that I put on green and, in about fifteen, twenty seconds, "green." He was never wrong. Sometimes he'd get it immediately. He said he could see the color in his mind. This confirmed my feelings that each color has a different feel, or texture. It was also the first indication that it was not only possible to infuse color energies into the life force with relative simplicity, but that it would affect consciousness directly. It demonstrated that the information communicated in the biocircuit was not a merely physical effect.

Using Substance Circuits at Home

It is easy to insert certain safe and effective substances in the biocircuit. This can be a wonderful tool for maximizing health and healing. Nonetheless, caution is advised. Because you are not ingesting the substance, it is easy to become careless. Don't. Never insert any substance in a biocircuit that you would not take orally with confidence.

I most often use the Eeman general relaxation circuit for inserting substances. This circuit gives a milder biocircuit effect than Eeman's optimal circuit, which is desirable with a powerful substance. Lindemann uses his universal relaxation circuit, placing his substances in the head to spine connection.

You can easily make a home-use substance circuit of copper (silk is impractical to clean after each use). Cut one of the wires of a copper biocircuit. Strip back the insulation for an inch or so.* The easiest method for preparing the substance for use in the circuit is to dissolve it in a glass container of pure water. (Certain substances, such as urine, don't need dilution, but most substances used in circuit are concentrated and need to be diluted.) After the substance has dissolved, insert the two copper ends into the water. The wires should not touch each other but should be submerged.

Remember that you don't need very much of a substance to get the full effect in a biocircuit. Begin by using small amounts, and increase the dosage slowly depending on your experience. The vibration or frequency of the substance will go directly into your energy field, so use discrimination in choosing substances for use in the biocircuit.

It is also important to limit the time in circuit with a substance. These agents (some more than others) can affect you very powerfully via the biocircuit. The length of time depends on the substance and your own reactions. Five to ten minutes is usually sufficient. I like to lie in circuit until I feel balanced. Then I drop the substance in the solution and lie in circuit for an additional five minutes. Don't stay in circuit with a substance if you begin to dislike the experience. Let your feelings be your guide.

Here are a few guidelines for using substances in circuit:

- *Choice of substances.* Almost any natural substance you normally ingest for a condition can be adapted for use in circuit. These include vitamins, urine, colored water, herbs, and homeopathic remedies.
- *Vitamins.* I find vitamin C to be extremely powerful and benign when placed in circuit. My first experience shocked me: it was more potent and energizing

---

* *You can also attach a small copper plate to each of the two cut ends.*

than I thought possible! Vitamin C in circuit boosts my energy level tremendously. I have also found it helpful in fending off colds and speeding up recovery. It is my experience that vitamins work with significantly greater effect when they are ingested before being inserted in the circuit. Perhaps the circuit signals the body to absorb what is orally ingested.

- *Urine.* Urine has been called "the body's complete personalized elixir." It contains detailed information about our own chemistry and imbalances. I have obtained very positive results when using my own urine in the circuit, and I believe the practice is very safe. Urine can be placed in the circuit without dilution. The traditional method described in ancient Hindu yogic texts is to use "the middle third" of the first morning's urine. This means discarding the first third and the last third of the urine eliminated. The morning's urine is considered the most potent, and of this the middle third is considered most potent and pure.

- *Herbs.* Herbs in a concentrated tincture are easier to use than dried herbs. Put a few drops (read the instructions on the bottle) in water and place them in the substance circuit. Herbs can also be made into teas and then placed in circuit. Try using herbal substances in circuit while you are taking them internally. The circuit may increase your results by signaling your body to utilize what you are ingesting orally. *Above all, be careful!* Herbs can be powerful medicine; taking the wrong herbs can make you ill. Use care in selecting herbs for your own use. We recommend that you consult a trained herbalist.

- *Homeopathic remedies.* These are obvious agents

for substance circuits. Simply dissolve them in water and place in the circuit. Homeopathic remedies are already a vibrational force. They are healing substances that have been so diluted or refined that only their essential vibration remains. Remember, *homeopathic remedies are medicines*. They should be treated with care. Homeopathic doctors train for years to be able to evaluate an individual's constitution and prescribe an appropriate homeopathic remedy. *Casual use of these medicines could have negative consequences.*

- *Allopathic drugs.* All drugs should be treated carefully, in or out of the substance circuit. They can be extremely potent. If used in circuit, make sure to minimize your time. Eeman found two to five minutes very powerful. Cut down the recommended oral dosage, starting with a quarter dose. I have found that aspirin taken only in circuit successfully relieves headaches.

- *Colors.* Colors are simply light vibrating at different speeds. The effects of color on the system can be heightened through the use of the biocircuit. Each color has a different feel, texture, and use. It is particularly important to understand the effects and purposes of each color before using it for healing purposes. I recommend you consult a color therapist or color therapy book before experimenting (see bibliography entries for Amber, Birren, Gimbel, and Hunt).

By the way, you can duplicate Peter Lindemann's color experiments very simply at home. There are several ways to use color with the biocircuit:

1. Place the color, in the form of a theater gel, between two pieces of silk (or copper, if that's the medium you

are using) and connect it into the circuit. You can do this while you shine the same color on your body.
2. Shine colored light on your body while lying in circuit.
3. Place "colored water"—pure water placed in a glass of the desired color and left in the sun for an hour—in the substance circuit.

You can use all three methods simultaneously. Whichever method or methods you use, the biocircuit will heighten and intensify the effects of color therapy.

Notes

1. Eeman, *Cooperative Healing and Reaction of the Human Body to the Frequencies of Drugs*, p. 14.
2. Powell, *Healing by Auto-Induction*, pp. 12–13.

Chapter 6

The Intelligent Trance and the Total Energy Body

Biocircuits readily induce a peculiar state of deep relaxation. Eeman described the sleep induced by the biocircuit as especially rejuvenating and "more refreshing than ordinary sleep." Lindemann playfully refers to this deep slumbrous state as "the zone," a middle state between deep sleep and the waking state. I have coined the term *intelligent trance* to describe this deeply relaxed condition.

This intelligent trance is a state of both body and mind, one in which the boundaries among body, emotion, and mind become permeable. In fact, this state promotes intercommunication among all the many levels of the body-mind.

There exist many useful "maps" of our subtle anatomy, both ancient and modern. These provide ways of understanding the coexistent realities of our emotional, mental, psychic, and spiritual lives. To frame the rest of our discussion, we need a general model of the subtle anatomy of human beings.

Esoteric Models of Life Energy

Most ancient cultures were aware of the life field surrounding the human body and all living organisms. Shamanic cultures all over the earth have long acknowledged psychic and auric dimensions of existence. Healing disciplines that predate the Bible, including folk medicine of all cultures, use laying on of hands to transmit healing energies. And all the great ancient civilizations, from the Mayan to the Egyptian, were highly developed in their sensitivity to nonphysical dimensions of energy and used this understanding in both their healing arts and their religious practices.

Chinese and Ayurvedic medical traditions have a five-thousand-year history of treatment based on a view of health that incorporates various levels of subtle energy. Acupuncture, t'ai chi, and yoga are systems for stimulating and balancing subtle life energies.

The simple description of the energy body that follows draws on Hindu terminology. Although there are many models and each is unique, the system I use here is in general agreement with Chinese, Japanese, and other Oriental models.[1] Some subtle anatomies identify many sublevels within each level described here. As Peter Lindemann says, "Ultimately, there is a continuum of experience which rides out octave after octave after octave of subtlety." For the sake of clarity, we use a simple model.

The Hierarchy of Subtlety

According to this understanding, the human body-mind is a hierarchy of energy that is stepped down by degrees through various levels of subtlety. Consciousness gives rise to life energy, which gives rise to the body—not the other way around. That is, the body's electrochemical processes do not "produce" consciousness. The subtlest levels are most senior.

In the various traditions, each of these levels is referred to as a *body, sheath,* or *vehicle.* The core of the being is consciousness itself, and these energies are like clothing around it. The physical body is a vehicle for consciousness, a sheath around the core of the being. In the same way, the subtler levels of energy are like layers of clothing around consciousness itself, which is infinitely subtle. The outermost, or grossest, layer is the physical body.

What level of energy moves through the biocircuit? It seems that *all* levels are affected. The biocircuit can access the entire continuum of conscious energy that we are. Our experience of moving energy in the biocircuit involves relatively gross etheric energy, but some biocircuit phenomena involve higher astral levels.

The Etheric Body

The etheric body is the grossest level of subtle energy, just subtler than the physical body. It is almost totally transparent and extends only a few inches out from the physical. It is closely identified with the electrical force field surrounding us and is the first and densest of the several fields of force that make up the composite emanation called the *aura*.

The etheric body plays a key role in the biocircuit phenomenon. It controls the reception, assimilation, and transmission of life energy throughout the physical body. It is directly related to the emotions and to the nervous system. The etheric body is the link between mental processes and the physical body. Breath is the primary way we affect this dimension of our being, both emotionally and energetically.

We notice etheric energy in the form of electromagnetic changes, sensations of moving energy, emotions, and changes in our breathing patterns.

Astral Levels

Subtler than the etheric is the astral body. The astral body is divided into two sheaths, the "mind" sheath and the "intellect" sheath. The mind sheath includes the ordinary conscious mind of the waking state, the subconscious, and the unconscious. The intellect sheath comprises higher mystical experience, spiritual understanding, and the basic assertion of ego and the will.

Together, the mind and intellect sheaths constitute the astral body. This astral body is described by clairvoyants as extremely vaporous and pervading the whole physical body.[2] Unlike the etheric body, it extends up to several feet beyond the physical body and is composed of numerous changing colors. Some biocircuit phenomena relate to the astral body. This body is extremely changeable and mobile, because it is directly linked with thought forms and emotions that are fluid and instantaneous. It is within this body that we see the phenomena of telepathy, astral projection, and visions.

Astral energy registers on two levels. Lower astral energy is experienced as memories, mental images (both visual and auditory), new information, and attitudes. At the higher astral level, we experience any of a wide spectrum of paranormal phenomena. These range from psychic phenomena such as telepathy and mediumship to exalted mystical states, visions, and experiences of cosmic consciousness.

The Causal Dimension

The highest body in this hierarchy is the bliss sheath, or causal body, where we find the fundamental root of the individual, consciousness itself. This sheath is small and located near the center of the body close to the physical heart. This is where all these sheaths, or bodies, originate. This sheath is the very source of life itself, the heart, whose origin is Atman, consciousness itself, the undifferentiated True Nature of every being.[3] There is no duality at this level, and therefore no experience or description is possible.

The Importance of the Intelligent Trance

From the point of view of our total energy body, the biocircuit's intelligent trance cannot be considered merely a state of mind. It is a profound state of body-mind integration. As a person relaxes and participates fully in the biocircuit experience, the flow of life energy becomes prominent. This experience overcomes the tendency to focus exclusively in mental, emotional, or gross physical impressions.

In the waking state, these different levels of the being seem separated and distinct. As psychiatrists can attest, it ordinarily takes hard work for us to find the memory or emotion that corresponds with a physical tension or ailment. However, the same life force animates mental, emotional, and physical processes. These processes are not radically separate or even altogether distinct. When the life force flows more fully, when its flow becomes predominant—as when we lie in a biocircuit—the obstructions to its flow in the form of latent memories, emotions, and physical tensions become more easily noticeable. Once noticed, they can be more readily released.

More than any other single factor, it is the *dissociation of our functions* that is partially suspended by the biocircuit's intelligent trance. Perhaps the flow of energy *integrates* the being at various levels. And perhaps in this intelligent trance we are made relatively whole, healed from the habitual divisions between body and mind, emotion and thought, body and emotion, and conscious mind and higher psychic sensibilities. This offers a useful circumstance for creativity, conscious self-discovery, and personal growth.

This intelligent trance helps open up the boundaries among deep levels of the being—psychic, mental, emotional, and physical. And this is an essential feature of human creativity. Artists, poets, and creative scientists have for centuries reported receiving inspiration through imagery while in unusual states of consciousness. The pioneer of biofeedback, Elmer Green, linked fringe states and hypnagogic imagery not only to personal growth and the development of supernormal abilities, but also to all forms of human creativity.* The biocircuit's intel-

---

* *With Alyce Green, he wrote, "reverie, hypnagogic imagery, dreaming and creativity are closely related. Various designations have been given to the state we call 'reverie'—for instance, the 'fringe of consciousness' (James, 1950), the 'pre-conscious' (Kubie, 1958), the 'off-conscious' and the 'transliminal mind' (Rugg, 1963), and 'transliminal experience' (MacKinnon, 1964)." Elmer and Alyce Green,* Beyond Biofeedback *(New York: Delacorte Press, 1977), n.p.*

ligent trance is a bodily integrated fringe state, one that enhances multidimensional awareness so that intelligence begins to penetrate into many otherwise hidden levels of the being.

When we fully allow this multidimensional flow, we move into levels of psychic sensitivity ordinarily excluded from our waking awareness. In this respect, the biocircuit is a facilitator. With its help, we can more easily contact dimensions of ourselves that are ordinarily inaccessible. Such work always requires disciplined effort, but the biocircuit facilitates it significantly.

Thus, biocircuits can be used as tools to enhance or promote nonordinary states of consciousness. The Czech-American researcher Stanislav Grof argues for the value of these nonordinary states as potentially "conducive to emotional and psychosomatic healing, personality transformation, and consciousness evolution."[4] Grof has researched nonordinary states for more than thirty years, first through clinical studies using psychedelic drugs, and more recently via nondrug therapies. Together with his wife, Christina Grof, he has systematized nondrug therapeutic techniques for entering into nonordinary states of consciousness. Prominent among these techniques are breathing, the use of music, and the use of imagery.

Biocircuits can be used to ease access to a wide range of nonordinary states. Grof has classified nonordinary states of consciousness comprehensively, dividing them into "perinatal" and "transpersonal" categories. Biocircuits can be used for "deep work," which involves accessing Grof's "perinatal" experiences. These are primal emotional confrontations that can be compared to vivid déjà vu recollections of the birth process, and even of life in the womb. They can be intensely painful and equally intensely euphoric or idyllic.

Biocircuits can also be used to enhance psychic sensitivity and aid people in entering into mystical states, experiences Grof classifies as "transpersonal." In this category he includes a wide range of experiences usually considered "mystical" or "spiritual." These may range from experiences of "oneness with life and all creation" to "past incarnation experiences" to "visits to other universes and meetings with their inhabitants." They are generally euphoric, and rarely painful or negative.

Grof contrasts both types of experiences with our "ordinary" state of consciousness in their potential to catalyze and quicken the process of personal growth. He argues for the value of nonordinary states in the context of therapy or skilled supervision. But he values both the perinatal and the transpersonal categories. Whether the individual's emotional experience is positive or negative, Grof sees nonordinary states as potentially transformative and far more powerful than verbal psychoanalysis.

Compared with other techniques for producing nonordinary states (such as psychotropic drugs, hyperventilation, sensory deprivation, etc.), biocircuits are an extremely *gentle* influence. Rather than producing a dramatic break with ordinary states of consciousness, biocircuits promote a *continuity* between ordinary and nonordinary experiences. This is their unique value. Used alone or as an adjunct to other techniques that produce more exaggerated influences towards nonordinary states, biocircuits can help us learn to live in a more inclusive reality, one in which the barriers between ordinary and nonordinary experiences can be crossed at will.

Visualization: Relaxation

The following visualization is an excellent way to release yourself from agitated energy or insomnia when you want to fall asleep. You can practice this with or without the biocircuit, but the biocircuit will deepen the experience. Not only will it help you to fall asleep quickly, but your sleep may be very restful, deep, and refreshing. You may find yourself moving into an unusually deep slumbrous state that seems to stand on the border between the waking state and deep sleep. This is the intelligent trance typical of the biocircuit experience.

1. Relax each part of the body, beginning in ascending order.
   a. Begin with the toes. Feel them relaxing. Let all tension go from that area. You can even say to yourself mentally, "My toes are getting completely relaxed . . . they are relaxing . . . they are relaxed totally." As you say this to yourself, *feel* the toes relaxing and letting go.
   b. Proceed from there all the way up the body. The feet, the ankles, the calves, the knees, the thighs, the groin, the genitals, the stomach, the chest, the shoulders, the arms, the hands, the fingers, the neck, the jaw, the mouth, the nose, the cheeks, the eyebrows, the eyes, the forehead, the entire head—all relaxing completely. Either visualize the body parts relaxing or, if this is difficult, use the mental affirmation ("my . . . is getting completely relaxed . . ."), or both together. Let go of all tension in every part of your body.
2. Now that your whole body is very relaxed, let it go. Imagine that if you let your body go completely, it would be carried by energy. Keep letting go, more and more deeply and profoundly. Imagine that your body is floating in energy.
3. Now that your body is floating in energy, imagine the energy itself. There is a golden light pervading and surrounding your body. Visualize this light. Feel the warmth of it. Feel your entire body floating in this golden light. Feel or imagine that your body *is* this light. Allow yourself to breathe and float in this energy. You may feel this energy radiating from your entire body. You may feel your body tingling, or you may become unaware of your body altogether and feel as if you are this energy alone. Relax deeply into this feeling.

Exercise: Breath and the Biocircuit

Although it is not necessary to manipulate the breath while you are in a biocircuit, breath can and does play an important part in your biocircuit experience. In general, it is sufficient simply to notice your breath and the changes that occur with it during your time in the circuit. But because it is principally with our breath that we can deliberately affect the etheric body, breathing can enhance the biocircuit experience. With a simple breathing exercise, we can heighten our experience of the energy circulating in circuit.

The breathing exercise we recommend is very gentle. It uses our normal breathing patterns, assisting us toward fuller breathing. It harmonizes the system and is useful for sensitizing us to the life force.

Preparation

Find a quiet place to set up your biocircuit. Always practice breathing exercises near a source of fresh air, either outdoors (but out of direct, hot sunlight) or near an open window. Always practice breathing exercises on an empty stomach, waiting at least one hour after a meal, so that your life energy will be available to your entire body and not concentrated in digestion. You can practice this exercise without the biocircuit. In that case, perform it in a sitting posture, taking care that your spine is fully upright.

Your tongue should rest on your hard palate, just behind your front teeth. This ensures that the circle of the life force in your body is complete. This technique requires only balanced and equal breathing, without strain, through both nostrils. Last, and most important, as you perform this exercise, assume that your whole body—physical, etheric, mental, and psychic—is already floating in and pervaded by the universal life energy.

In the beginning, practice this exercise outside the biocircuit in order to learn to perform it naturally, without reading the text. Then, when you are comfortable with the exercise, begin using it while lying in the biocircuit. Take note of any differences you feel performing it in and out of the biocircuit.

Technique

1. Relax your entire body while lying in the biocircuit. Feel that you are gazing into and resting in a field of all-pervading life energy.
2. a. Inhale *slowly*, taking as much air into your lungs and as much life energy into your whole body as you can. *Do not strain or force the breath beyond your capacity.*
   b. Direct the passage of air against the back of your throat. This area should be relaxed and fully opened. You might try lowering your chin slightly to help open your windpipe.
   c. Breathe from your heart to your vital center, the region around your navel. Allow your feeling to expand fully with your breath.
   d. Feel your whole body—visible and invisible, head to toe—becoming full, like an inflating balloon. Notice the movement of your breath, first filling up your vital center by pressing your solar plexus up, then swelling your abdomen. Feel how the breath fills your entire body, from your throat to your perineum, finally permeating even your head, legs, and feet with vibrant force. *Make sure not to strain or force the inhalation.*
3. Relax, opening your entire body as much as you can to the feeling of unlimited energy. Hold the inhalation for a few seconds, but only to the point of what is natural. Enjoy the intensity of life force and life feeling between the two phases of the breath cycle. Notice what you are

feeling. Has your biocircuit experience changed or been augmented? Are there any signs of life-energy movement in your body (e.g., energy perhaps moving up the spine, circulating around the chest area or down to your toes; are there tingling sensations; warmth)?

4. Exhale *slowly* and deliberately, releasing all the air inhaled through both nostrils.

   a. Feel that you are releasing not only physical wastes, but all emotional obstructions and negativity, bodily tensions, and disease.

   b. Exhale for about as long as you inhaled, and exhale about as much breath as you inhaled.

   c. Pause for a few seconds before inhaling. Notice again what you are feeling in the biocircuit. Do the energy sensations change from exhalation to inhalation? Is the feeling of energy simply augmented with this practice? Or is there no change at all in your bodily sensations?

5. Repeat this cycle again and again, for ten to fifteen minutes. Follow the process fully. You should feel the entire process as a cycle of equals, in which the whole body is engaged with feeling.

6. While you engage in this exercise, you may have many experiences. You may want to get up and break the biocircuit. Perhaps the energy will be too intense. Or perhaps you will feel a lot of emotions or old memories. But *do not abandon the practice.* Simply relax deeper into whatever experience you are having. You may not feel uncomfortable at all, but may instead feel very blissful—or perhaps you will feel nothing at all. Simply stay with whatever you feel and relax into that.[5]

Notes

1. The simplified subtle anatomy provided here is loosely based on that of Da Free John. See *The Illusion of Relatedness*. For an extremely detailed contemporary Western description of the subtle anatomy, see Gerber's *Vibrational Medicine*.
2. Saraswati, *Science of Soul*, pp. 83–183.
3. Da Free John, *The Illusion of Relatedness*, p. 105.
4. Grof, *The Adventure of Self-Discovery*, p. 3.
5. Da Free John, *Conscious Exercise*, pp. 200–202.

Chapter 7

Talking to the Unseen Body

Have you ever wished you could communicate with your body the way you can speak to another person? If your body itself would listen to you in a very open way, you might be able to help it realize that it doesn't really need desserts (or cigarettes). You could show it how to relax into athletic activity more gracefully or even help it become more self-confident and courageous in fighting disease. Biocircuits can relax and open up deep levels of the body so that it listens when we speak to it. They can increase the effectiveness of various methods of self-programming ranging from hypnotherapy to biofeedback techniques and including visualization and affirmation practices.

Visualization Exercises

Westerners have recently rediscovered visualization exercises. Today visualization practices are attracting special interest and emphasis, but they have been a key element in shamanic practices since prehistory. Since ancient times, they have been an important part of Eastern meditative practices. Such Oriental esoteric traditions as Taoism, Tantra, many advanced yogas, and the Siddha tradition have long used the power of creative visualization.

Since Eeman, the power of visualization exercises has been reconfirmed dramatically by Westerners in many different quarters. Today, visualization exercises, imagery, and imagery work are used widely by humanistic psychologists, notably in the Italian psychologist Roberto Assagioli's "psychosynthesis," as a means of engaging the participation of the whole person in self-discovery and in desired emotional or psychological changes.

These exercises are also used extensively by cognitive and cognitive-behavioral therapists as a means of engendering physically based changes, such as breaking addiction to cigarettes. Visualization exercises have even been used, with impressive results, as a means of strengthening the immune system in cancer patients. U.S. Marines have been trained to maximize effectiveness by programs incorporating visualizations. Several series of sports-training videotapes that have recently come into wide use and commercial distribution depend on the efficacy of passive visualization. And active (internal) visualization exercises have proven their value as an important element in the training regimes of various Olympic and professional athletes.

Eeman's "Conscious Suggestion"

Through his work with patients and the relaxation circuit, Eeman had learned that the mind could positively affect bodily well-being. Accordingly, he developed a therapeutic system of visualization techniques that he called *conscious suggestion*.

Eeman proposed to influence the physical health of an individual via transmitted thought. He felt that this technique could directly affect the emotional or psychological and therefore the physical well-being of an individual. In fact, for Eeman, the two were inseparable, since optimal health depended on the amount of energy available to the physical body. Energy bound up in emotional or mental contractions meant that the amount of physical energy was reduced.

Although Eeman gave instructions on how to employ this technique in a solo circuit, he preferred to use it in cooperative circuits in order to boost the available energy supply. An individual suffering from a malady, such as weakness and enervation, would lie in circuit with a group of generally six or more healthy individuals. All participants would concentrate on the same mental image—for example, the subject in glowing health, running a hundred-yard race on a hot, sunny beach and defeating five formidable opponents.

Eeman emphasized the fact that such images had to contain many specific details; successful conscious suggestion depended on these details, he contended. First, the object had to be desirable and functionally attainable. Second, the subject had to clearly desire the results. Third—and very important—the image had to be extremely specific and vivid, involving as many senses and physiological functions as possible. And by performing the exercise while relaxed in a biocircuit, the subject would increase the energy available for the desired results.

According to Eeman, this technique, while drawing upon the support of others, enables the subject to participate in his or her own healing. A subject relatively weak in visualization ability can be assisted by the others lying in the cooperative circuit. People with similar difficulties would not be included in the circuit, but the inclusion of someone with special strength (such as a brilliant sprinter) would, Eeman believed, serve to enhance the effectiveness of conscious suggestion.

Eeman monitored the breathing, pulse rates, and body temperatures of subjects in circuit as a way of assessing the impact of the conscious suggestion at the level of the body itself. When he asked subjects in circuit to visualize themselves running, swimming, or doing other strenuous exercise, he found that they exhibited the appropriate heart, lung, skin, blood pressure, and other changes that might be expected from such activity, yet they rarely twitched the muscles that would actually be involved. When the biocircuit was broken, the physical signs ceased.

This led Eeman to an obviously false conclusion: that visualization exercises are effective at the level of the body *only* when the individual lies in circuit. Today we know that visualizing a flawless gymnastics workout produces dramatic improvement in later competitive performance. But Eeman's central finding seems most certainly true: the biocircuit powerfully amplifies the body's reception of visualized programming.

Eeman believed that conscious suggestion had more powerful, more integrating, and longer-lasting effects than hypnosis, largely because it engaged the conscious participation of the subject.

Biocircuits and Biofeedback

Dr. George Fritz, supervisor of Biofeedback Services at St. Luke's Hospital in Bethlehem, Pennsylvania, employs biocircuits (which he calls *polarity plates*) in his biofeedback practice. His practice focuses on stress-related diseases with physical symptoms that are a direct result of nervous tensions. Fritz helps his patients learn to control through various biofeedback exercises their stress-reaction levels under a wide range of stressful circumstances. Sometimes he asks his patients to lie in a biocircuit while performing these exercises. According to Fritz, "The biocircuit acts as a booster, in addition to facilitating sleep and relaxation."[1]

At the last two annual conferences of the Biofeedback Society of America, Dr. Fritz conducted biofeedback demonstrations using the biocircuit. He took volunteers from the audience (which was made up of the society's members). Fritz conducted exercises, in which members of the audience participated, both in and out of the biocircuit, and found that the volunteers in the biocircuits consistently described an intensified subjective experience of the biofeedback exercises.

Dr. Fritz's reports corroborate Eeman's claims that biocircuits enhance the effectiveness of visualization exercises. It is Fritz's hypothesis that the state induced by the biocircuit allows his suggestions to be received by "the deep body-mind," allowing the whole brain to absorb the material effortlessly.

I believe that this heightened receptivity to visualization exercises is due to the intelligent trance state of body and mind created by the biocircuit. In this state, the boundaries between body and emotion and mind become permeable, helping the person to experience visualization more fully and deeply at the level of the bodily being.

The evidence suggests that the biocircuit can be a valuable tool for other professionals who use visualizations, imagery work, affirmations, or positive programming to facilitate personal change, particularly psychologists (especially sports psychologists), hypnotherapists, biofeedback practitioners, and rebirthers.

Exercise: Two Visualizations

Do the following visualizations while lying in the biocircuit. Spend a few minutes relaxing in the circuit. After you are relaxed and starting to feel the movement of the life force, begin the visualization exercise. Don't worry if you can't actually "see" an image or mental picture. Simply use your imagination in whatever way feels right to you.

Visualization: Healing the Body

In this exercise, you use the biocircuit to relax deeply and visualize the healing of your body. You can use this to visualize a general healing and magnification of health and well-being, but this visualization was written specifically to be used to visualize the healing of a specific injury or ailment.

1. Lie in the biocircuit until you feel very relaxed and pleasantly warm. Visualize a golden light surrounding your body. Feel both your body and the entire environment pervaded and floating in this warm, golden light. Allow yourself to breathe and float in this energy. As you visualize this golden light surrounding your body, feel that it is soothing and healing. Relax and enjoy this energy.

2. Either by mentally verbalizing the question, or simply by feeling the meaning of the question, ask the part of your body that needs healing if it has a message for you, if there is something you need to do, learn, or hear from it. Relax. An answer may come to you in your feeling. If you receive one, follow it as best you can. It is the body's message. Don't worry if no answer comes; simply continue with the visualization.

3. Feel this golden, healing energy pervading and surrounding you. In order to make use of this healing energy fully, you need to first breathe away all obstructed or negative energy. It is easy to do this by imagining breathing in this golden healing energy on inhalation, and then *visualizing the release of all obstructions on exhalation.* Do this cycle at least three times, or until you feel that the problem has been released, concentrating your attention on the *release* or exhalation of all toxins, negative energy, and physical obstructions, especially in the part of you that needs healing.

4. Now, using your breath once again, direct healing energy to the indicated area. Do this by *feeling or visualizing that, upon inhalation, you are receiving the nurturing power of the universal life energy.* Let that loving energy fill your entire body. Again, do not strain or force your breathing. *With the exhaled breath, direct that energy, through the power of your visualization and feeling, to the area that needs healing.*

In addition, when you inhale, allow the wounded area to practice receiving this nurturing and healing energy directly, as if that part of your body were directly breathing this life energy. With exhalation, feel that part of you radiantly glowing, full of energy, healed and loved.

Initially, in this phase you intentionally direct healing

energy to the area with your exhaled breath. But after several repetitions of the breath cycle, you may feel moved to visualize the area glowing and radiant, already full of health, upon exhalation. Be sensitive to and trust what you feel. Feel free to adapt this healing exercise to your needs. Try this exercise outside of the biocircuit. Notice any differences. Does the biocircuit help your powers of visualization? Is your concentration improved during the exercise while in the biocircuit, or are the images more potent?

5. *This is the most important phase:* having completed the healing visualization, relax any expectations about what your healing will be. Trust that you have done your part to heal the injured area. Have great faith that you will be given whatever is necessary and appropriate for your growth, happiness, and spiritual understanding.

Visualization: The Inner Athlete

Eeman used an exercise similar to this one for stimulating motor function. It aids efficient and effective athletic performance. The exercise requires that you first relax in the biocircuit. Then you can begin to use it creatively. This exercise offers a basic model, but you will enjoy it most if you improvise. "Inner" athletic activity is extremely enjoyable. Not only is it fun, and in a real sense stimulating and invigorating, but it can also improve actual athletic ability!

The exercise outlined here will work especially well if a friend reads it to you while you lie in the biocircuit. If that is not practical, I recommend that you read it over several times until you can remember it, and then rehearse it mentally as you lie on the biocircuit. At first it may take you up to half an hour to do the whole exercise, but with practice you'll be able to do it efficiently in only a few minutes. In the exercise, I outline breaks during which I suggest that you observe your pulse

110

or breathing. These are optional, and in any case they should take only a few minutes.

If some of the details included in this description are not suited to you, simply substitute those that are attractive. Try this exercise every night—before bed is a good time—for two or three weeks (ten days is a minimum for practical improvement to take place), and note the results. You can easily tailor this visualization to suit your own needs, for example, applying it to swimming, gymnastics, or other activities. You can also apply these same principles to specific goals, such as the improvement of a particular function (such as throwing a ball or swinging a tennis racquet). The main requirement for an effective image is that it be polyideistic—that is, involving multiple ideas that engage a number of your senses.

1. As you lie relaxed in the biocircuit, recall the sense you have of your body at its peak condition, probably between the ages of twenty and twenty-five. Allow your images to be as real, vivid, and lifelike as the memories can be.
2. Take yourself on a vacation to a warm seaside resort. Envision yourself in your swimsuit, standing with friends at the top of a good hard beach about 150 yards from the shore. Enjoy the sun, breeze, and sea, and look forward to your swim in the ocean with real pleasure.
3. Just as you are about to move off toward the water's edge, one of your friends challenges everyone to a race to the sea. On your mark, get set—go!
4. Run as fast as you can. At the quarter distance, you're third . . . run hard to pass number two at the half distance . . . then struggle fiercely to challenge the leader, catch up to him, and, after a terrific fight, leave him behind in a tremendous final burst of speed. (You might want to pause at this point to notice your breathing, pulse rate, etc.)

5. Get into the water, fight your way through the breakers, feel the stimulating blow each wave gives you, take a dive, and swim: feel the rhythm in your strokes, gradually increase their power, challenge yourself to a few bouts of real speed; and then get back to shore. (Pause here again if you like.)

6. In your own private place, take off your bathing suit and with your roughest towel, to get the maximum skin stimulation, rub every inch of your body in detail as hard and as fast as you can: the back, then the front of your trunk; your neck, face, scalp; your arms and hands to your fingertips; your legs and feet to your toes.

7. Lie down on the warm sand and sunbathe. Feel the heat of the sand, air, and sun. Let the energy from the sand, air, and sun pour into you through your skin, course through your blood, suffuse and vitalize your brain, all your organs and limbs, your nerves, muscles, and bones. Let every single cell, like a battery, charge up with sun energy and *enjoy it*. (Pause here to observe the physiological effects, if you like.)

8. After a while, visualize yourself falling asleep on that beach. Imagine the deepest, soundest, and most recuperative sleep nature can give you continuing for hours. Since this is only your imagination, you cannot get a sunburn. Sense this sleep and then watch your body fast asleep on that beach, as though you were outside it.

9. Imagine yourself, after hours of the marvelous sleep, gradually coming back to consciousness, amazingly fresh and vital, and feeling intensely the most irresistible urge to stretch. Imagine yourself stretching every limb in your body, again and again, to the fullest extent, and rubbing your eyes, and yawning vigorously as healthy children do on waking, first while still reclining, and then standing up.

Eeman sometimes used images such as this one in cooperative circuits. Since different people have different vivid memories, he felt many individuals enhanced each other's images. Try this visualization (or one of your choice) while a friend performs laying on of hands (see chapter 9) while you lie in a solo circuit and *both* of you hold the image. Another option is for several people to hold the same image together while touching the person lying in circuit; this can help to enhance the visualization of the person in circuit. Still another alternative is to have one person narrating the images above while everyone else visualizes them during laying on of hands.

Notes

1. Dr. George Fritz, in a telephone conversation with the authors.

Chapter 8

Listening to the Unseen Body

Our bodies can tell us secrets about ourselves that our minds have buried and forgotten. Emotions and memories stored in our bodies can be the keys that unlock liberating insights and self-understanding. I have used the Lindemann silk circuit with the intention of reaching emotional material held deep within my own body, and I have been amazed at how powerfully it facilitates this kind of work.

Many physical problems have emotional tensions as their root causes. Medical science acknowledges the role of the mind and emotions in causing high blood pressure, hypertension, ulcers, and so on. Many physical and psychological therapies see imbalances in the emotional being, owing to trauma or repressed emotions, as the cause behind most or all physical ailments. They argue that acute energy imbalances tend to become chronic patterns of imbalanced life energy. These chronic imbalances are reflected in emotional problems and in patterns of muscular tension and "armoring." Ultimately, energy imbalances find their expression as patterns of bodily degeneration and disease.

Deep work, such as Reichian therapies, Rolfing, Hellerwork, rebirthing, and bioenergetics work, all aim to make lasting changes in the deep patterns underlying psychophysical stress. In bioenergetics work, as described by Alexander Lowen, people make contact with emotional content by assuming several specific "bioenergetic" postures and breathing deeply and rapidly. One of the primary bioenergetics postures is to stand, knees bent slightly, bent over at the waist, with hands hanging toward the ground. In this posture, extra blood flows into the head. If the posture is maintained for several minutes, the knees begin to quiver. If the deep and rapid breathing is sustained, the heartbeat accelerates. This bioenergetic posture simulates the bodily experience of intense emotion. In some forms of bioenergetics therapy, people use the postures in combination with speaking emotionally charged words or phrases, such as "No!" or "Why?"

Fifteen years ago, I did some bioenergetics work and experienced some powerful emotional cartharses. Afterwards, I felt suddenly more comfortable with my body and my emotions, and I felt that this work had been of real value. When I used the biocircuit with the intention of doing deep work, I did not imagine that it would stimulate dramatic emotions in the manner of bioenergetics. I had lain in biocircuit configurations many times, and always had relaxing, gentle experiences.

I was amazed to discover that the biocircuit is an extremely potent tool for contacting deeply held emotional material. It functions more gently than the bioenergetics postures. From my experience, bioenergetics exercises force intense emotions of anger, sorrow, or fear, even if they are not ready to appear on their own. Since such emotions are nearly universal, doing this is frequently useful, but in the work I did in the biocircuit, the only emotions I experienced were those that emerged naturally from the patterns of tension within my body and energy.

When I did this kind of work in the biocircuit, all I "did," apparently, was breathe deeply, a little bit more quickly than usual. Deep and feeling breaths are an important "trigger" for the emotions. As I breathed, I simply intended to allow emotion to come to the surface. Whatever I felt, I allowed. I intended not to react to any emotion, and if I did react, I allowed my reaction. My intention was simply to be present with whatever I felt, and my intention was to allow myself to feel levels of experience that were deeply buried below my everyday consciousness.

It is not easy to be so completely present. Meditation practice helps to make us sensitive to how "unpresent" we are and helps us learn how to get out of the way of what is. Deep work in the biocircuit is something like meditation in this way. I found that it proceeded naturally when I was simply present in this very vulnerable way.

When I did this, I gradually allowed the intelligent trance stemming from the biocircuit to assume control. My body relaxed more and more deeply, and heavy, odd twitches occasionally went through my legs and spine. After a while, waves of emotion began to surface. Deep feelings of grief and sorrow came up very naturally and gently on their own. As I allowed them, I wept, and I felt from a depth of vulnerability that seemed primitive, echoing back from my infancy, or even before. As I allowed myself to simply experience these emotions fully, they came to a point of completion on their own. Then new feelings arose, deepened, and passed.

When I finished such sessions, I felt joyful and euphoric, and my expansive mood seemed to reside in every cell of my body! I found this deep emotional work to be extremely intelligent and economical. It enabled me to deal directly with my unfinished emotional agenda precisely in its own order of priority. The experience was self-empowering, gentle, and more natural than the bioenergetics work I had done years before.

I was especially amazed by the power of the biocircuit's influence. Outside the biocircuit, I couldn't duplicate the profound bodily depth of my experience. The biocircuit's gentle deepening of my attention seemed to open gates within me. I felt as if dimensions of my being had suddenly become intercommunicative and that long-lost connections could be made naturally at the level of feeling.

Lindemann's Experience

Peter Lindemann did his early biocircuit work with Eeman's copper relaxation circuit. Using magenta light, which he shone on himself while lying in the copper circuit, Lindemann was able to extend his viable treatment period for hours. In lying within circuit for these longer periods, he found that after he had succeeded in resolving the superficial stress of the day's activities, deeper tensions and stresses would surface. By working consciously to experience and release these stresses, he was able to purify his system of various deeply held patterns of stress and imbalance. He continued these longer sessions over a period of time. When he developed the silk biocircuit, he was able to extend these sessions significantly.

Emotionally charged memories would surface in the circuit, but Lindemann found that the release of old patterns did not always necessitate the reemergence of traumas. Sometimes powerful releases took place without any specific memories accompanying them at all.

"Using the biocircuit, I was ultimately able to pull an incredible amount of stress out of my body." Lindemann's health problems were among the motivations of his research, and he had considered iridology—reading the patterns in the inside of the eye as a reflection of the whole body's health—as a way of understanding his condition. His irises showed five concentric "nerve cramp rings." After lying in circuit for longer periods of time, Lindemann saw these rings begin to clear up. Eventually, he was able to clear up all five stress rings, simply by lying in circuit.

Lindemann did not merely go to sleep during his long sessions in the circuit. By his account, he lay in circuit "with the intention of encountering deep levels of stress and imbalance." He stayed in circuit for a long enough time to pass through his superficial levels of stress, and when he encountered his deep material, he "consciously released it."

Eeman's Myognosis

Eeman, too, developed a technique for accessing and releasing deeply held emotional/physical patterns. In this technique, which he called *myognosis*, the patient lay in circuit and progressively relaxed the body—first the feet, then the legs, thighs, hips, and so on, leading up to the face and head. As the body relaxed, Eeman would notice body movements or breath variations. Frequently, he would ask the patient to breathe more deeply, making him or her more conscious of breath inhibitions. He would manipulate the patient's arms, legs, or head, drawing the person's attention to areas of muscular tension. His techniques consistently led to the "emergence" of repressed traumatic memories.

After a memory had "emerged," Eeman would guide the patient through repeated relivings of the emotional trauma. The memories would be relived both forward and, interestingly enough, *backward*. Eeman felt that reliving traumatic memories backwards was a very powerful therapeutic technique. He theorized that in the interim since a traumatic event, we remember the incident many times, but always forward. This process familiarized us with the memory and somehow diminished its power. But when we approach the experience in reverse, we encounter it anew, with none of its power diminished. With repeated reliving, repressed emotional memories lose their power, and the patient becomes reintegrated but without the previous pattern of emotional and muscular contraction.

According to Eeman, "Loosening of the physical tensions often means a 'spring-clean' of the mental processes, clearing debilitating 'debris' from the subconscious regions of the mind. The resultant sense of freshness is a wholesome thing to experience, and it inevitably stimulates the mental functions. This in turn is reflected in an increase of physical well-being."[1]

Aubrey Westlake, in *The Pattern of Health*, described Eeman's concept of myognosis as follows:

1. *Any trauma, especially a psychological one, tends to set up a nervous muscular tension in some part of the body, which tension is unconscious, and a vicious cir-*

*cle tends to be set up. To resolve this it is necessary to
make the tension conscious. As soon as this is done
the tension goes and there is complete relaxation. Any
tendency for the tension to return can be dispersed by
conscious thought.*

2. *Removal of the neuro-muscular tensions tends to an
   emergence of the buried memories which first produced them, together with the emotional content,
   which consists of the psychic energy repressed with
   the memory.*

3. *This released energy is now available to the patient for
   his restoration, i.e., healing; or it can be added to the
   total available energy of the body.*

4. *This psychic energy has a polarity which can be used
   therapeutically. . . .*

*One result of this muscular relaxation or "Myognosis," as he
called it, is "emergence," by which Eeman meant a vivid and
full reliving of the buried and unconscious original experience
which had produced the tension and trauma. This, Eeman
maintained, was real psycho-analysis, as in the course of teach-
ing relaxation he would also enable the patient to gain relief
from his hidden complexes. . . .*

It is of interest to note that Eeman used to accomplish in
comparatively few sessions what it might take an ordinary
psycho-analyst years to uncover, *if he managed it at all; and
the result would be nothing like so good [emphasis added].*[2]

In *Cooperative Healing,* Eeman tells several dramatic stories in which patients lying in circuit suddenly recall early
childhood traumas—with long-lasting therapeutic benefit.
Anne Atkinson, a British radionicist, corroborates Eeman's stories as well as Westlake's high regard for his practice of
myognosis:

I was very interested in his relaxation techniques and asked

119

if I could attend a meeting at Baker Street to watch him at work—it was usually a small group—6–8 persons, excluding Mary Cameron and himself. He would select a person, put them on a couch [which was wired with a relaxation circuit] and relax them from the feet upwards. Most of us had no idea how tense we were. On the second occasion he relaxed me I was struck by a very curious sensation on the left side of my face. Suddenly Mr. Eeman said, "The left side of your face is paralysed. Can you tell me why?" Without a second's hesitation, I heard myself reply, "My father caught me smoking and slapped me across the face." Eeman said, "And you were ashamed." "—Yes!" The sensation in my face eased away and I have never been bothered since.[3]

Eeman achieved remarkable results with his myognosis, largely because he became a highly skilled and sensitive therapist. But Eeman did not leave behind detailed descriptions of his technique.* We do not know exactly how he provoked "emergence" of old memories with breath work and bodily manipulations while the patient lay in circuit. Thus, to our knowledge, no full and usable methodology survives from his work.

The Intelligent Trance and Deep Work

Body-centered psychological therapies all describe the interrelationship between emotional traumas and patterns of muscular tension. Some therapies attempt to release bodily

---

* *A small volume,* Relax Your Way to Health, *by the British Naturopathic Doctor H. D. Cotton and with an introduction by Eeman, was published in 1954. It contains Cotton's description of some of Eeman's myognosis techniques and is illustrated with pictures of Cotton performing those techniques on one of his patients. The descriptions are somewhat abbreviated, but this volume may be of interest to therapists wishing to learn from Eeman's work with myognosis. In addition, two chapters in* Cooperative Healing *contain a more theoretical discussion of myognosis.*

obstructions directly, on a physical level. This can lead directly to powerful emotional releases. Frequently, the approach is made on two fronts at once. While working to release physically held traumas, the therapist will also address the emotional content itself through verbal conversation. Bodily tensions, emotions (both past and present), and personal memories are all addressed together, because they are inseparable. Each is simply a different octave of a single pattern of disturbance to a healthy energy flow.

It is important to remember that the life force is conscious. In fact, it is the essence of our awareness. In the areas where we are obstructed and tense, we are also unconscious. But the life force is not. By restoring a full and free flow of life energy, the intelligence of that area of the body reemerges.

In the state of relaxation induced by the biocircuit, the body and mind can more easily remember and reveal their mutually held secrets. The biocircuit helps bring suppressed emotion, hidden memories, and physical armoring to the surface. At the same time, it helps the body, emotion, and mind listen with particular sensitivity to one another. The restored intelligence of the freely flowing life force empowers our emotional beings, our bodies, and our hidden memories to speak, but also to listen.

It is important to emphasize, however, that the release of obstructions is real work that must be done consciously and responsibly. The biocircuit is not a substitute for this work, but an aid to it.

Biocircuits are not the only means for facilitating such encounters, but they are perhaps unique in their combined power and subtlety. Where some other approaches, such as bioenergetics, press quickly into the encounter with the emotional material, the biocircuit permits a more gradual encounter. Nonetheless, it is a powerful facilitator in that process. Thus, *the biocircuit promotes a high degree of conscious participation* in that encounter. This is its special advantage.

Deep work without the assistance of a therapist and done with the aid of the biocircuit requires time and commitment. It is probable that this kind of work requires particularly extended sessions in the silk biocircuit. Old patterns, if they are to be left behind, must be encountered and released. The biocircuit can be used as a tool for this process. But if there is to be real change, a new freedom must be discovered and a conscious and responsible choice made to exercise that new freedom. Otherwise, new unconscious choices will replace the old ones, and no valuable change will result.

Professional therapeutic sessions may be one of the most important applications of biocircuits, and may offer one of the most creative opportunities for further research. Since Eeman did not leave behind explicit instructions for therapeutic techniques with biocircuits, any professional work with biocircuits in body-centered therapies must be integrated with the work of already skilled practitioners. But therapists who already do this kind of work will find that the biocircuit can be a powerful aid in the process of opening patients to repressed memories and feelings.

These applications stand at the frontier of the new field of biocircuitry. They deserve serious attention and new research. Today, personal growth and therapy is far more sophisticated than it was during Eeman's lifetime. Experiential psychotherapies such as Reichian and neo-Reichian therapies, bioenergetics, primal therapy, Lomi work, and rebirthing (or "circular breathing") are examples of the humanistic and transpersonal approaches to body-centered therapies that can employ biocircuits in new and powerful ways.

Exercise: Using Biocircuits for Deep Work

Deep work should not be engaged in casually or trivially with difficult emotions such as grief, sorrow, anger, and the sense of abandonment or engulfment. Most often, confronta-

tions are best engaged in with the help of a qualified therapist. A loving and supportive environment can make a tremendous difference to the success of this kind of intimate confrontation. *Anyone with even a minor degree of emotional or psychological instability should engage the help of an experienced therapist before doing deep work.*

Some people, including Peter Lindemann, have done this kind of work in biocircuit successfully without the help of a therapist. It is not as a rule *always* inappropriate to do this kind of work alone. Some people may feel comfortable and confident about exploring these deeply intimate and personal experiences with a spouse or close friend. Thus, in the interests of thoroughness, I include the following exercise for performing deep work. But for many people it *is* inappropriate to engage in these explorations without the help of a trained and skilled therapist. Therefore, I recommend caution; please approach deep work responsibly.

1. *Relax.* Relax deeply, as you would in any biocircuit session, suspending expectations. Let the biocircuit's "intelligent trance of body and mind" help begin to reconnect your emotion and life energy and body feeling.
2. *Open.* As you relax, feel as though you are opening up. Allow *everything* to arise. There is nothing that "should not" arise—or that "should" be expected. Allow and notice any tension in your body and any emotions.
3. *Breathe.* Once you have "sunk into" the biocircuit experience, begin to breathe more deeply and rapidly than you normally would. Open as you breathe. Continue to allow everything to arise. Breathe into the top of your chest. Breathe into your heart. Breathe into your belly. Breathe into your genitals. Lean back your head and open your throat as you breathe.
4. *Feel.* As you notice and allow tensions or emotions, just

"be with" your feelings. To "be with" them is simply to feel, to be present. There is no need to exaggerate emotions. There is no need to suppress them. There is no goal. Let them be. Let the experience be one in which there is space for feelings you have not been able to allow before. To feel is not the same as to *try* to feel. If you feel boredom or frustrated expectation, be with that boredom or frustration. What is the emotional quality of it? How do you feel it? Where is it in your body? Keep breathing, and feel. There is no need to manufacture emotion. Your feelings are already yours. If you are really present, the feelings that are ready will surface.

5. *Release.* As the emotional content arises, let it go. Notice whether you are tending to hold on to your feelings and invest them with special meaning. Allow yourself some humor about your own life's pathos. That pathos, those memories, are only residues of your past. Let your past appear, but then let it slip back into the past. Let it all go. On your exhalations, release everything, trusting that you do not need it anymore. You don't need to hang onto any of it.

6. *Keep returning your attention to the process.* You may become bored if strong emotions or memories do not arise, and your attention may drift. If strong emotions do arise, they can be distracting, and in the next moment you may find yourself thinking about the incredible experience you just had—instead of being present, breathing, feeling, opening, and allowing. Whether it is boredom or excitement that distracts you, bring your attention back to the exercise at hand. Keep breathing and feeling, keep opening and allowing. Don't worry about your drifting attention, but when you notice it drifting, bring it back to the process you are involved with.

7. *Give it time.* This process, especially if it is not facili-

tated by a therapist, can require a lot of time. Even as
many as several hours at a session may be necessary.
The unearthing of deep content may come only after a
long period of intense opening and relaxing. So, if nothing impressive happens for a while, do not take your
inevitable impatience too seriously. Just breathe, relax,
open, and allow.

Notes

1. Cotton, *Relax Your Way to Health*, from the preface by
   Eeman.
2. Westlake, *The Pattern of Health*, pp. 65–66.
3. Anne Atkinson, in a letter to the author, July 1987.

Chapter 9

Invisible Octaves of Enjoyment

In the biocircuit's intelligent trance, we can travel into new territory, taste subtle pleasures, and discover new powers of mind. We can cross the boundaries that usually prevent us from having psychic perceptions and transpersonal experiences. Life energy rises into level after level of subtlety. At first we are likely to feel a rather gross etheric level of energy moving in our bodies. But later we may begin to feel subtler energies and experience subtler phenomena.

Psychic Sensitivity Begins with Energy Sensitivity

The biocircuit will not "create" supernormal experiences, but it will facilitate them. Usually, the individual must consciously participate in the process. Mystical experiences have occurred spontaneously in circuit, but this is unusual, and shouldn't be expected. It will usually take persistent, disciplined effort over time, usually under the guidance of a skilled teacher, before you achieve higher mystical experiences. *Nevertheless, the beginnings of psychic sensitivity can be awakened via biocircuits with relative ease and then steadily extended.*

For many people, the words *psychic sensitivity* suggest an extraordinary gift that one either has or does not have at birth. But psychic sensitivity is a natural capacity of human beings, even those not born with an extraordinary gift. It may develop into a dramatic ability, but for most people it begins in more ordinary ways.

Most psychic phenomena originate in the *pranic* or *etheric* dimension of our being. (Higher psychic capacities engage the astral being as well.) This dimension exists as a field of force or energy that connects us to the natural world and to a universal energy that extends beyond our bodies into the whole universe.

Sensitivity to the etheric dimension can be developed easily. In fact, it is used by most people every day. It begins with sensitivity to our intuitive, psychic, and emotional interactions with others and the natural environment. As this capacity develops, we begin to notice that life energy is continuous with emotion. Negative emotions disturb the energy body. Positive emotional states such as love, pleasure, or exaltation are expressions of radiant, healthy life energy. We begin to discover that healthy emotion is inseparable from the rest of health.

This sensitivity can extend further, and as it does, our inherent psychic capabilities naturally awaken and, through continued practice, blossom. For some, that may mean experiencing ESP, telepathy, and clairvoyance, while others may simply find themselves awake and clear, naturally open and aware of energies in nature and their personal relations. Along with the use of appropriate exercises and strong intention, the biocircuit can be a powerful tool for quickening etheric and even astral sensitivity.

Eeman's Telepathy Research

Eeman reported experiences that he explained as serendipitous. Two subjects linked together in a cooperative circuit would fall asleep. Then, simultaneously, they would stir, stretch, and open their eyes. One would comment, "Strange, I just ate before I came here, but I kept dreaming about a huge dinner!" And the other would say, "You must have been picking up my dreams! I'm famished!"

Such scenes occurred again and again. Subjects picked up a wide range of information from each other. Eeman came to understand and expect such responses when they involved physically based information such as drunkenness or hunger, but he was still surprised to find that emotional and even purely mental information was commonly shared. It wasn't until 1925 that Eeman's work with his "antisceptic battery" satisfied him that true telepathic communication was fostered by cooperative circuits.

The "antisceptic battery" (so named because Eeman frequently used it to silence his skeptics) was Eeman's switching device for cooperative circuits. He wired all the subjects directly into a central box, and then used this box to remove an individual subject from the cooperative circuit or rearrange the juxtaposition of particular individuals, all without the subjects' knowledge. Eeman found that sensitive subjects could unerringly tell when another individual entered or left the circuit and could even identify the individuals who were adjacent to them in the circuit.

Once he became convinced that the circuit fostered the telepathic exchange of information, Eeman wanted to prove it scientifically. He began by studying the mind and its effect on the body. Since thought is inherently subjective and difficult to observe objectively, he initiated his telepathic study by investigating the relationship between thoughts and observable physical signs. Through this analysis, Eeman hoped to create an objective system and methodology.

He divided thoughts into categories: those involving *color and sound*, those involving *temperature sense*, and those involving specific *physical activities*.

Through extensive observation of subjects wired separately or together in the biocircuit, Eeman established a system that enabled him to correlate thoughts with physical manifestations. Eeman's system for thought was remarkably comprehensive. Through extensive experimentation, he demonstrated that thoughts do tend to be accompanied by specific bodily signs. And he found that these bodily signs are magnified with the biocircuit. Thoughts involving colors affected the breath, and thoughts involving physical activities manifested themselves in physical activity. Thoughts about running would produce muscular tightness in the legs, deepened breathing, quickened pulse rate, and increased bodily heat. And all such physical signs were clearly and dramatically increased if the subject lay in a biocircuit.

Cooperative circuits increased these physiological responses even more markedly. Even those whose minds wandered showed the appropriate bodily signs if the others in the circuit with them concentrated on a particular thought. Sometimes people in a cooperative circuit not holding the thought could guess the sender's thought.

Eeman was now convinced that telepathic communication occurred readily among individuals wired together in cooperative circuits. His experience had already provided him with an overwhelming store of anecdotal evidence. But random telepathy is "wireless." Could the circuit also enhance the *reception* of telepathic signals broadcast from others not directly "wired in"?

In order to devise verifiable "wireless" tests, Eeman began a deep study of telepathy. He identified three factors usually present in successful telepathic communication:

- The liberation of latent force, usually through heightened emotion (frequently associated with danger, shock, or death);
- Lowered objective attentiveness in the receiver;
- A state of affinity between the sender and the receiver.

Eeman then conducted a long series of experiments designed to enhance the likelihood of successful telepathic transmission. He tried to provide the three factors listed above or adequate substitutes for them. Eeman didn't want to shock or frighten his subjects, so he couldn't create actual heightened emotionalism for his experiments. As a substitute for this telepathic factor, Eeman engaged a whole crowd of telepathic "senders" for his experiments instead of a single individual. Also, on the hunch that the circuit's wires might act as antennae, Eeman used additional wiring in an attempt to increase the subjects' receptivity.*

To decrease objective attentiveness in the receivers, Eeman placed them in circuit and instructed them to relax. To create a state of affinity between sender and receiver, Eeman arranged to have at least one relative of each receiver in the "audience" of senders.

Then Eeman arranged for the crowd of senders to think a particular thought for several minutes. He and several assistants would monitor the breathing patterns, bodily temperature, muscular contractions, and other physical reactions of the receivers. Then he would ask the receivers to report their subjective experiences.

Eeman conducted volumes of such experiments, meticulously recording the results. He concluded that more than three-quarters of the receivers demonstrated physiological reactions appropriate to the images on which the senders concentrated. The majority were aware of these reactions; many even mentally interpreted the image that was being sent. Control experiments in which the receivers did not lie in circuit produced dramatically different results. Eeman was satisfied that the relaxation circuit fostered telepathic reception.

Out-Of-Body Experiences and Channeling

The deeply relaxed intelligent trance state promoted by the biocircuit is very similar to certain trance states that are used in entering into superordinary experiences. In particular, the procedure for out-of-body experiences calls for deep relaxation

---

* *Eeman did find that with lengthened wires, the subjects reacted sooner and their physiological reactions were more vigorous. Also, there was a further increase in some subjects' reactions if 150 feet of carefully laid wire was substituted for 25 feet of haphazardly laid wire.*

into a state in which "the body is asleep and the mind is awake." The biocircuit is extremely conducive to precisely such states. Yogic literature describes the *tandra* state and the *nidra* state — sleeplike trance states that can be used in the development of unusual mystical experiences. Biocircuits may be especially valuable in facilitating the efforts of those already engaging in astral travel or mystical practices involving explorations into such states of consciousness.

One psychic practice that has become particularly popular in the past few years is "channeling." It is frequently called trance channeling because most approaches to channeling require the channeler to enter into a specific trance state. As with any psychic experience, there is more to channeling than entering into a trance, but achieving a deep trance can be an important part of the process, and biocircuits are an effective and powerful aid for inducing the deep state necessary for channeling.

The Joy of Subtle Experience

Discovering that you are a field of energy can be a delightful perception. In the biocircuit you can understand yourself as a play of energy and actively *be* that play of energy. *Being* energy can be very revealing, instructive, and liberating. The laws of energy are laws of movement and flow. On the physical plane, effort, fear, anger, knowledge, and ownership seem to be all-important tools of power and survival. In the domain of energy, however, they only obstruct the flow. The domain of subtlety rewards us for letting go, relaxing, enjoying, feeling, and surrendering.

Biocircuits can teach an important lesson about pleasure. We experience pleasure when feeling flows without obstruction. When feeling encounters a limit, that feels bad. Although the world is full of pleasures, it is also a constant play of limits, which frustrate pleasure. The physical world is full of dangers, impositions, and offenses. People, places, and things are constantly bumping into us. But in the energy dimension, nothing "bumps" into anything. The energy dimension is fluid. Like emotion, it can change in a moment. In fact, emotion is the "flavor" of energy. In those planes, everything flows relatively freely, the edges of experience are softer, more tender, and more open.

We all live in the midst of the limitations physical existence imposes. As I began to balance my life by participating regularly and pleasurably in the energy dimension, I discovered that a profound process of healing had begun. Suddenly I was taking regular time to swim in a dimension where there were no solid limitations and feeling, if I stayed with it, could flow freely. So we can use biocircuits to learn about the pleasures of the energy dimensions, pleasures that are explored inwardly rather than outwardly.

Over time, I developed a certain taste for these subtler pleasures. They are very refined, esthetically elevated, sometimes even exquisite. You enjoy them in the mood of surrender and love and gratitude. Because you are engaged in them in a safe environment, you can open yourself until you are extremely vulnerable, and in that condition, your sensibilities are keener, far more capable of fully savoring the profound esthetic experience of positive emotion itself, than on the physical plane.

Learning from Subtlety

Da Free John has used biocircuits for almost a decade. As a spiritual realizer, he is, among other things, an accomplished yogi and psychic, and he has observed and confirmed the effectiveness of this technology. He recommends biocircuits to his students as a tool for developing energy sensitivity and for balancing the body prior to meditation.

He has suggested that we use biocircuits to develop an expanded understanding of ourselves, a psychically awakened perspective, in which we discover that our bodies and minds are not merely physical, but are also in fact a whole spectrum of living energy:

We should basically feel and perceive that we, as well as others with whom we are associated, are Radiant. This is not a matter of imagination. It is true. If you become doubtful and want to prove that you are energy, use pranayama screens [Da Free John's term for the Eeman biocircuit] for a few minutes. Remarkably, they will communicate to you that whatever else you are, you are a field of energy. Energy is running through your hands, your fingers, your back, your head. You will discover that you can change your sensations simply by causing those currents to run differently. Anyone who does this even once will gain a sense of himself that he perhaps did not have before.

By using the pranayama screens, you create a circuit that is different from the circuits being created by your tensions. The body thus receives energies in areas that have been closed off and you gain a sense of balance or rejuvenation. But you also begin to notice something about yourself as energy. That is very important to notice. Eventually you will notice it without using pranayama screens. You will begin to enjoy such bodily sensitivity to the flows of energy that you will enter into the right relationship to these energies in every moment. You will enjoy the capacity to transcend your negative circuitry and live in a state of fullness of energy without tension. Thus you can effectively learn the lesson from pranayama plates, but then you must take on that disposition psycho-physically at all times.[1]

Da Free John is suggesting that we use biocircuits to expand our sensitivity and that we extend that sensitivity into our whole lives, whether we are lying in the biocircuit or not. Thus, the biocircuit serves as a biofeedback mechanism, enabling us to become responsible for increased sensitivity, vitality, and balance. It is a practical tool through which we can become conscious of and sensitive to our esoteric anatomy—our energy bodies. On the basis of what we notice in the biocircuit, we grow in awareness and responsibility.

I believe this process of *learning* from the biocircuit experience is the key to some of the most interesting applications of the technology. Eeman's experiments tell us that people lying in a biocircuit demonstrate dramatically increased telepathic receptivity. This is interesting, and it is probably worth experimenting with. But if you want to increase your telepathic capacities, you probably want those capacities to persist when you are *not* lying in the biocircuit. This requires, first, that you become sensitive to how you have changed during the biocircuit experience and, second, that you become capable of intentionally exercising the capacities awakened by that experience.

If you achieve this goal, your use of biocircuits can become the basis for a profound integration of body, emotion, and mind. You can gain not only psychic capacities, but integration and balance. The intelligent trance of the biocircuit experience is reintegrative: it works to heal the dissociation of our busy minds from our armored bodies, forgotten emotions, and latent psychic and intuitive powers. If you can learn from biocircuits how to heal that dissociation in daily life, you will have realized a truly rare capability.

Exercises

Three exercises follow: one for psychic sensitivity, one for children, and one for laying on of hands. Each involves extending sensitivity and functional strength into new areas. For individuals who wish to develop specific psychic abilities, biocircuits can be used in conjunction with practices directly tailored to the particular ability. Some of these explorations are extremely difficult, and it may be best to approach them with the guidance of an accomplished psychic or mystical teacher.

Exercise: Psychic Sensitivity

This simple exercise is designed to help sensitize us to our energy bodies. It is very similar to the healing visualization in chapter 7, except it encourages us to relax, enjoy, and magnify this energy rather than direct it to specific bodily parts.

1. Relax as fully as possible in the biocircuit. When you are balanced and relaxed, visualize a golden light surrounding and pervading your body. Feel it as a soothing, nurturing force.

2. Now begin to engage your breath consciously to magnify this energy. Do this by imagining breathing in this golden light on inhalation and then, on exhalation, *visualizing the release of all physical, emotional, and mental obstructions, wastes, and negativity.* Concentrate initially on the release phase, performing this cycle at least three times, or until you feel the release phase is complete.

3. After completing your release phase, begin concentrating on the reception phase. Visualize and/or feel that you are breathing in this golden light. Allow its loving, nurturing energy to fill and pervade your entire body. Do not strain or force your breathing. With your *exhaled* breath, relax more deeply, allowing this golden energy to pervade every cell of your body. Continue this phase for at least three breath cycles (or longer), relaxing and feeling more deeply with each exhaled breath.

4. When this golden light has pervaded the cells of your whole body, visualize it pervading the brain, including all the deep recesses within the head and every convolution of the brain itself. This light is the same as your mind and your body. You are a single bright field of energy.

5. Visualize this light radiating from your body-mind out in every direction. Visualize it shining out into the

cosmos above you and down into the earth below you. The entire field of existence is a single matrix of living light, and you are not separate from it in any way.

6. Visualizing this universal matrix of intelligent living light, notice that you are in some sense connected to everything. You are simultaneous with all life and all mind. Notice how this universal interconnectedness of everything opens new possibilities. The universal field of intelligence, with which you are so deeply connected, can draw on information from anywhere. It can even manifest new possibilities. Surrender more deeply into that universal light and allow it to animate your body and mind. Open yourself to it, both to serving it and to receiving its gifts.

7. Magnify and radiate this feeling through several breath cycles. Allow it to reveal whatever it will reveal.

Exercise: Using Biocircuits With Children

Most children are naturally able to feel energy in their bodies. This is especially true of children six to twelve years of age (although the biocircuit can be used with children as young as four years old), as the energy dimension, including emotion, is developing and can be discovered and explored at this time of life. Using biocircuits can confirm and extend this natural sensitivity and is therefore highly recommended. It can also help children become sensitive to the difference between balance and imbalance, harmony and "crazy" energy.

Because young children often find it difficult to lie still for an extended period of time, we recommend visualization exercises in conjunction with the biocircuit. While the child lies in the biocircuit, the adult should tell the story to them, using simple language and vivid pictures. We have found these combined biocircuit/visualization exercises particularly helpful for young children in the following ways:

- in helping the child feel and learn about the etheric dimension;
- in balancing and calming the child;
- as an aid to internalizing the humanizing instruction you give your child. This is similar to the positive reprogramming that adults can do on themselves.

Gear your image toward whichever of these three areas you wish to emphasize (see the example below). We have found that for all visualization exercises it is important to direct the child's use of the breath in his or her imagined world. You might encourage this by enjoining the child to take a big, enjoyable breath to conduct the pleasure of the image throughout his or her whole body. This will help adapt the child's body to a condition of inherent pleasure. Or you might suggest that the child breathe out any "bad stuff" that may be in the way, either externally or internally. By using the breath, the child will integrate the image more easily while being helped to become more sensitive to his or her energy being. Periodically during the visualization, remind the child to breathe in this way.

The short visualization below will help reinforce positive and humanizing growth in children. It is intended to enhance their emotional/psychic sensitivity not only to themselves but also to others and to the natural environment. Exercises such as these orient children to recognizing, feeling, and enjoying their bodily sense of energy as the pleasurable sensation of the life force.

Say the following to the child while he or she is lying in a biocircuit:

Close your eyes, and take three deep breaths. Relax your whole body, toes to head. [You can go through a simple version of the relaxation visualization here if you desire.] When you are very relaxed, imagine that we are going to the beach, a beautiful beach full of warmth and sunlight.

We are in the car driving down the road, when suddenly the car stops! Are we going to get unhappy? Nope. Instead, let's give energy to the car by breathing out what is wrong with the car and breathing in good energy to the car. Breathe out.... Now, breathe in... and the car starts up again!

Now we're at the beach. Are we going to run crazy or are we going to get some toys and the lunch we packed and the blankets and towels? Right, we are happy to be here and there is lots of energy in our bodies. We are breathing that energy all through our bodies. And we are staying with feeling that energy before we play. Oooh, the sand is warm on our feet and it is squishing between our toes. Mmmm, and the wind is warm and blowing across our bodies and we feel so good and happy. We are just breathing that happiness and enjoying the sun and the waves and the smell of the ocean. Can you smell the ocean?

Now we join our friends, who are building a sand castle. Oh oh. Two people are fighting over the shovel and bucket. How does that feel? Right, not very good. Let's breathe out that bad feeling with one breath and radiate the feeling of love and sharing to them with the next breath. Now we go over to them and show them that they can share. Now everyone is happily building a fantastic sand castle. (And so on....)

You can also adapt the relaxation exercise for children. It will help calm them down and balance them. And you can adapt the psychic-sensitivity visualization for children as well. Have them breathe out bad feelings from their entire bodies—"breathe out the bad stuff"—and breathe in the radiant light, "good stuff," glowing over their entire bodies. Remind them to feel this light as happiness, in their hearts, and all over their entire bodies. And so on. . . .

Exercise: Laying on of Hands and the Biocircuit

Preliminary Exercise

This exercise begins by sensitizing you to the feeling of energy in your hands. When you perform this preliminary exercise, you are not lying in the biocircuit. You will experience your energy body through your hands.

1. Sit comfortably in a chair with both feet on the ground.
2. Hold your hands in front of you, palm to palm, with your arms relaxed, elbows slightly away from your body. Bring your palms as close together as you can without touching, perhaps an eighth of an inch apart.
3. Slowly separate your palms by about four inches, then slowly bring them back to their original position, an eighth- to a quarter-inch apart. *Do not allow your hands to touch, as this will break the circuit.*
4. Repeat the procedure of slowly moving your hands back and forth in front of one another *without letting them touch.* You can widen the distance up to six or eight inches. Continue this back and forth movement, very slowly and deliberately (see Figure 9-1). Be aware of any tingling or of the sensation of a build-up of pressure between your palms. Some people feel heat, others feel a vibration like a "buzzing," and still others feel an

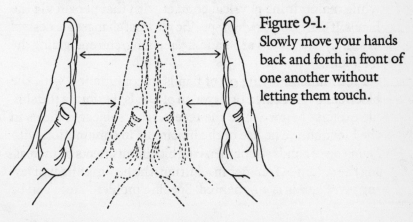

Figure 9-1.
Slowly move your hands back and forth in front of one another without letting them touch.

attraction between the palms that makes it seem easier to bring the hands closer together than to pull them apart. You may feel one of these or other sensations. Simply be attentive to what you do feel.

5. Finally, stop your hands at around six or eight inches apart and very slowly bring them together, stopping every two inches. Notice the pressure field you have built up, and slowly try to compress the field between your hands. You may feel this as a "bouncy" sensation.

6. Once you've felt this tingling sensation, rotate your hands circularly. See if you can feel the breaking of the tangible rays of force.

7. If, after completing this exercise once, you have felt no energy between your palms, try energetically rubbing your hands back and forth across each other several times quickly to stimulate the nerve endings and "wake them up." Then repeat steps 3 through 6.

Children ages five and up especially enjoy experiencing their energy body with this technique.

Laying on of Hands

Laying on of hands is a method of affirming, and even visualizing, the positive and desired changes on another's behalf while maintaining physical contact with that person via the hands. It can be done when specific physical changes are desired or simply as a means of balancing, relaxing, and energizing the recipient.

I recommend laying on of hands in conjunction with the biocircuit. The healer, or "layer on of hands," performs the simple exercise below while the receiver, or "subject," relaxes in the biocircuit. The use of the biocircuit in conjunction with laying on of hands strengthens the biocircuit effects by increasing the volume of energy. In addition, the healing effect of laying on of hands is augmented. Specific problem areas can be directly addressed with force and purpose. Also, the art of laying on of hands requires the recipient to practice relaxing and receiving in order to accept this additional healing energy. The biocircuit aids this process.

Energizing both the entire body and specific bodily areas requires the healer to intentionally radiate positive healing energy through the hands to the recipient. This intention is coordinated with the breath cycle, and anyone can learn to do it.

The receiver cooperates in this conscious and intentional act by relaxing in the biocircuit (although this method can be used without the biocircuit), closing the eyes, and feeling (or imagining) the life force surrounding and pervading him or her. The receiver then releases all negative conditions into this energy and affirms all the desired positive changes.

Figure 9-2.
The recipient relaxes in the biocircuit
while the healer performs laying
on of hands.

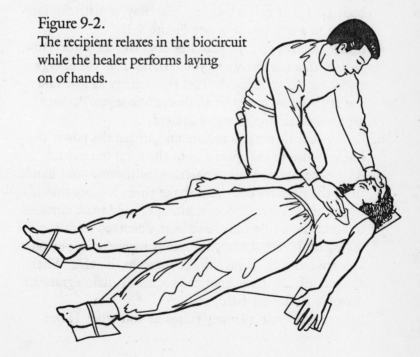

The following instructions are for the person performing laying on of hands, the healer:

1. Inhale and exhale from the vital region, the area just above the navel. Feel the fullness of life force there.
2. Close your eyes for a moment. Try to feel the energy surrounding and pervading your entire body. If you are unable to feel energy around your body, simply be aware of the energy in your hands. Then increase the energy in your hands by feeling and visualizing the energy in your arms and shoulders. Bring this energy in your shoulders and arms down into your hands by visualization.
3. Hold your hands, palms open, over a specific area on the receiver's body. You can place your hands on the person's head, heart, abdomen and solar plexus, or any body part that needs healing. You may, intuitively, feel drawn to a specific area (see Figure 9-2).
4. Inhale, feeling as if you are inhaling the life force. Now radiate this life energy to your friend. Feel the energy radiating via your hands. Feel this energy as love and the affirmative power of all desired changes. Perhaps even visualize the changes desired.
5. Exhale, continuing to radiate and affirm the power of life and love to that part and to the total individual.
6. As you complete your exhalation, withdraw your hands from the person's body and shake them loosely towards the ground or into space, shaking off any toxic energies or conditions that may have been absorbed from the recipient. Never shake your hands towards the person you are treating; always shake them to the side. When shaken off, any toxic energies naturally disintegrate and dissolve in the life field.
7. Repeat this cycle as many times as you wish. Never

inhale with the feeling of drawing negative or toxic conditions from the receiver; rather, always inhale with the sense that you are receiving the power of life.

8. At the end of laying on of hands, relax and breathe the life energy through several breath cycles with the feeling that all unhealthy conditions you may have picked up during this process are *completely* released with each exhalation, via the breath and all the body parts, into space.

9. Always wash your hands after performing laying on of hands, because running water easily purifies any toxic energies that may have been received during the session.

Notes

1. Rothemich, "Sing the Body Electric," p. 47.

Chapter 10

The One-Month Program for Life-Energy Enjoyment

Energy experiences and the pleasurable sensations of the life force moving in the body are our natural inheritance. If we cannot feel the life force, it is because we have "forgotten" it—and thus we can, quite naturally, "remember" it. In order to reclaim this natural inheritance, we need not become extraordinary. We need not sit in a cave or give up material pleasures. We need only become sensitive to this dimension of our existence and begin to enjoy and make use of it in our everyday lives. Biocircuits are not the only means of developing this sensitivity, but they are certainly a unique and powerful tool to this end.

It is my suggestion that, to increase energy sensitivity, you commit yourself to a program of regular, daily biocircuit use for one month. Although it is not necessary to follow this program to gain benefits from any one session with the biocircuit, a single month of regular use will greatly heighten sensitivity to the life force in most individuals. And in one month, someone who is already sensitive can make significant advances in deepening that sensitivity while balancing and enjoying the life force.

Whatever your level of sensitivity, your experience in using the biocircuit will probably be subtle, perhaps extremely subtle at first. Let that subtlety instruct your sensibilities. To make the best use of the biocircuit, you must learn from it. You will need to pay attention to very subtle feelings you may be accustomed to ignoring. And you will need to persist in regular practice over a period of time.

Developing sensitivity is a matter of personal discovery and free experimentation. Nevertheless, "rules" for the beginning use of biocircuits can be useful:

1. *Relax body and mind.* Begin each session with a series of deep breaths. Close your eyes. Consciously set aside your time on the biocircuit as relaxation time. While you lie in circuit, relax from whatever creative thinking or worrying you may feel impelled to do.
2. *Practice regularly.* At the beginning, it is very useful to commit to a regular schedule. Use the biocircuit after work if possible or before bedtime. If you use it only "whenever you feel like it," you may notice benefits but you will not allow it to instruct you fully.
3. *Suspend expectations.* Beginning meditators, like beginning practitioners of biofeedback and visualization techniques, frequently obstruct their own progress by judging their experience against a set of expectations. They tend to imagine either that they are more advanced than they really are or that they are failing. In general, neither assessment is true. Allow your experience to unfold naturally.
4. *Be aware of subtleties.* Your experience may begin undramatically. Perhaps you will merely feel drowsy at first, or perhaps you will—"coincidentally"—sleep more deeply at night. You may feel distinct sensations of energy movement or have dramatic relaxation experiences. Notice them all, large and small. We have supplied a checklist (Table 10-1) to aid you in systematically noticing subtle signs of growth in your use of biocircuits.

The Six-Stage Process of Energy Sensitivity

Use these stages (and the associated signs, listed at the end of the chapter) as a guide. Your process may not follow this scheme exactly. In any case, simply allow it to unfold naturally. This stage-by-stage process can occur quickly—even in one session—or slowly, over the course of many weeks.

Table 10-1

A One-Week Progress Chart

Sensations	Day 1	Day 2	Day 3	Day 4	Day 5	Day 6	Day 7
Urge to stretch							
"Waves" of intensity							
Warmth, general relaxation, fuller and deeper breathing							
Intensification of energy imbalances (usually within the first ten minutes)							
Drowsiness, sleep							
Harmonization of energy imbalances; sense of integration							
Tingling sensations in hands, feet, sacrum, or neck							
A felt current of energy flowing in the body (note where and how you feel it)							
Lightness, roundness, wholeness, nonidentification with physical body, sense of the etheric body							
Fullness of energy in the upper body (Eeman configurations)							
Energy aligned centrally along the spine (Lindemann circuit)							
Intense pleasure, joy, ecstasy							
Sense of beginning to "lift out" of the body; out-of-body experiences							
Other							
Other							

Signs

There are six stages associated with the biocircuit experience, four stages of energy sensitivity, and two more stages involving advanced extensions of that sensitivity. The last two stages may require more advanced and extended use of the biocircuit. They are listed here for reference only because some sensitive individuals may experience these stages within the first month. For most individuals, the formal one-month program will probably stop at stage four.

I have listed the signs associated with these stages; the beginner who is not used to noticing subtle experiences may be reassured that "it's working" by identifying the signs. By understanding the stages, you will know what kinds of experiences are possible. Not everyone experiences all these signs. You may even have experiences not included on this list. Simply be aware of what you do feel. I have included only some of the most common signs. You may notice any of these signs or a combination of them at any time during the one-month period of biocircuit use.

A reminder: If you are a beginner using either of the Eeman circuits, and if you feel tense, agitated, irritable, and unable to tolerate the circuit for more than a few minutes at a time, you may have reversed polarity. Try reversing the handles. If this relieves you, then this is the correct relaxation circuit wiring for you.

The One-Month Program

Which Medium to Use

This one-month program is designed to be used with either silk or copper. You can also switch between the two media at any time. If both are available to you, I recommend beginning with the copper, because it produces the most easily perceptible experience. Even if you are still having trouble discerning any sensations of energy with copper, switch to the silk after two to three weeks. Some people are more sensitive to the silk than the copper.

Which Circuit to Use

You can begin this program with the Lindemann circuit or either Eeman circuit. It is best to use the same circuit every day for three weeks. In week four you will alternate between the different circuits.

The checklist in Table 10-1 will help you keep track of your progress over one week. Photocopy it for a one-month's supply. Each day review the checklist and mark the appropriate box or boxes that best describe your biocircuit experiences. If you noticed sensations not listed, write them in the extra boxes provided. This will help you notice the progression of changes throughout the month and also help to validate your subtle energy experience itself.

Progressing Through the Stages

Treat this program as something like a self-taught correspondence course in energy sensitivity. This is a course with no tests or teachers, only stages that proceed like progressive lessons. Don't let the programmatic quality diminish your enjoyment. Once you have fully mastered the first stage, you will have developed a foundation for the second. You will miss much of the value of this program if you skip through it too casually. Engage each stage *fully* before moving on to the next. Notice the signs of each stage as they naturally appear.

This program is designed to be useful for people who aren't particularly aware of their sensitivity to life energy. If you are already familiar with life energy, the early stages will be familiar to you but this program may be useful to you nevertheless.

Please maintain the discipline of lying in the biocircuit *every day* for a full month, even if your progress is rapid. This kind of extended, regular use will enable you to engage the biocircuit experience and explore its possibilities in a significant way.

Even if you do not feel certain that you have completed a stage, move on after a week or so. Some people (such as myself) take a long time to feel certain that they are really feeling life energy. Don't let doubt slow you down. During the month, pace yourself so that you move through the first four stages.

Preliminary Exercises

Before you begin the formal program, a few preliminary exercises will help establish a "hint" of the direction in which your sensitivity will develop:

- *Exercise 1.* Begin by lying down in a cool room with your arms by your sides and your feet apart. Notice your breathing and body temperature and be aware of any physical sensations. After five minutes, cross your feet at the ankles and interlock your fingers, placing your hands on your stomach. Remain relaxed in this position for another five minutes. Again be aware of your breathing and body warmth. Do this exercise at least one time before beginning the formal program.
- *Exercise 2.* Before you fall asleep at night and after you have settled down in your bed, lie on your back and place your right hand on your lower abdomen and your left hand behind your head. Cross your left ankle over your right. Check to see if you feel more relaxed and warmer. Do this exercise for several nights before you fall asleep. This is a natural biocircuit. You can do it any time you feel stressed or tired without the biocircuit device.

The Program

Here is the one-month program. Stay at each level for about a week and then move on. In this way, you should move through the first four stages of the program during the month. If you experience signs associated with later stages, don't be concerned. That is perfectly natural. In general it is best to stay with the program.

On the other hand, if your experience seems to be progressing rapidly and if you feel that you have fully completed and explored a stage before the week has passed, go ahead to the next stage. To account for this, we have included instructions for six, not just four, stages of growth in the program.

Stage 1: Deep Relaxation or Sleep

The first step in the energy sensitivity process is to become aware of the difference between being relaxed and being tense. At the beginning of the program, simply notice the differences in your breathing and body temperature and distinguish between states of relaxation and tension. Relaxation can go far deeper than most of us experience. Allow yourself to become so utterly relaxed that you may even become drowsy or fall asleep.

Stage 1 Signs

- Drowsiness, sleepiness.
- Pleasurable warmth.
- Relaxed breathing, fuller and deeper breathing, lowered pulse.
- Occasional surges of sharply deepening relaxation.
- Particularly deep and restful sleep.
- An urge to stretch at the end of a biocircuit session.

Stage 1 Exercise

Lie in the biocircuit for at least ten but preferably thirty minutes every day. The best time is after the workday or before bed. Remember, if you lie in the circuit before bed, you will probably fall asleep. This is a good use for the biocircuit, but it does make it difficult to be aware of what occurs during that time. Don't worry about your thoughts; thinking is not a problem. Instead, simply bring your attention to your body. Observe the way your body feels. Watch for changes. If you notice any sensations, such as tingling and imbalances, simply bring your attention to them and observe them. Do not try to change these sensations. Only notice them.

Stage 2: Balance, Harmony, and Stress Reduction

We move on now from simply noticing whether or not we are relaxed to beginning to become sensitive to the *process* of relaxation itself and how we feel after we use the biocircuit. In this stage, we become more aware of the difference between imbalance and balance. Notice all the physical changes that happen during your time in the biocircuit. Were your imbalances magnified initially? Observe the entire process of stress reduction.

Stage 2 Signs

The signs associated with stages 2 and 3 overlap considerably, so I have grouped them together. They are listed under stage 3. The most physical, or "gross," of these signs, such as tingling sensations or stiffness in the joints, may appear first. The subtler ones, such as sensations of expanding beyond the physical body, may tend to develop later.

Stage 2 Exercise

Continue using the biocircuit every day, but add the visualization exercise for relaxation from chapter 6. This exercise will help you enter into deeper relaxation in the circuit. The ability to relax deeply is essential for reaping the benefits of the circuit and also for becoming aware of the movement of the life energy. Do the exercise once through; then remain relaxed and aware in the biocircuit until you feel satisfied the experience is complete.

Stage 3: Recognizing Signs of the Energy Body

The energy body is continuous with the physical body. You are experiencing its signs all the time. In this stage of the program, you learn to *recognize* these signs. You may even feel *new* evidence, such as fullness in the upper chest or a strong current of energy coursing through your body. At first you will probably notice more humble signs, such as tingling in the hands and feet or sensitivity to the "wave effect" of the biocircuit.

Signs of Stages 2 and 3

- Intensification of energy imbalances. You become highly aware of disturbing feelings in your body. These are disruptions of the natural energy flow. After a time these imbalances even out and harmonize.
- If you are using copper: awareness of the experience definitely ending, usually after 10 to 30 minutes.
- Stiffening of elbows and other joints from the increased life flow.
- Tingling sensations in the hands and/or feet.
- The experience of the biocircuit coming in "waves," with times of intensity alternating with lulls.
- The jerking or twisting of the entire body or any of its parts from the increased energy flow.
- In copper circuits, sensations of heat in the hands.

- Sensations of energy coursing through any area of the body.
- Fuzziness of the physical boundaries of your body. It becomes difficult to distinguish your body from the energy surrounding it.
- Expansion of your physical body. You identify with your energy body more than with your physical body. This can also make you feel as if you are resting in a "sea of energy."
- Feelings of lightness, roundness, wholeness. These are extremely pleasurable, even ecstatic, sensations.

Stage 3 Exercise

Continue your daily use of the biocircuit, beginning your sessions with the relaxation exercise. Add the simple breathing exercise described in chapter 6.

Stage 4: The Different Qualities of Life Energy

In this stage, you pay attention to many different qualities possible in the life force. Here you experiment with all three circuits and place substances in the circuit. Until this point, the one-month program has been possible with a copper or silk two-part Eeman biocircuit. The exercises in stage 4 require a three-part biocircuit, and they even suggest using both copper and silk as well as a copper circuit with a broken line suitable for inserting substances into the circuit. If you do not have all the equipment called for in these exercises, simply do the exercises that are possible with the equipment you do have. In stage 4, you will concentrate on increasing your sensitivity to the subtleties of the life current.

Stage 4 Signs

In the Eeman relaxation circuit:

- Fullness in the upper body, especially the chest.

- A strong current of energy in the upper body.

In the Eeman optimal circuit:

- Sensations similar to those sensed in the general relaxation circuit but greatly intensified.
- A strong sense of energy, perhaps felt as a current aligned vertically along the spine.

In the Lindemann circuit:

- A sensation of energy in the feet, even tingling.
- A feeling of energy running "centrally symmetrical."
- A very strong sense of the energy running vertically—up, down, or in a steady intensity—along the spine and possibly even down to the feet between the legs.

Stage 4 Exercise

Continue to use the biocircuit every day, but begin experimenting with different types of circuits. Try the Lindemann circuit (or the optimal Eeman circuit, if you are already using Lindemann's circuit) for at least three days in a row. Try Eeman's basic relaxation circuit and see if what you feel differs from what you feel in the optimal Eeman circuit. Try some of the additional circuits described in chapter 13. You can also experiment with substance circuits. The substances I suggest are vitamin C and the first morning's urine. Both substances are potent, energizing, and safe.

The Advanced Stages

The basic One-Month Program ends with stage 4. Stages 5 and 6 are included for two reasons: (1) certain sensitive individuals will progress rapidly during the month and will enter into these stages naturally, and (2) others may wish to continue their growth in the program beyond a month. These two stages offer opportunities for extended exploration. Either of them may take more than a week to complete, and both of them can be fruitfully examined for much longer than a week.

Stage 5: Life Energy as Continuous With Emotion

In this stage, you begin to discover the dynamic unity of the integrated body-mind. All the moving energy you are feeling in the body is a more physicalized expression of the moving energy that expresses itself emotionally. Negative emotions such as fear, sorrow, or anger powerfully disturb the life energy. Positive emotional states such as love, pleasure, exaltation, or esthetic awe are expressions of magnified, healthy life energy.

Stage 5 Signs

- A sense of how emotionally "bruised" you really were at times when your attention was superficial and when you would have said you were feeling "fine."
- A sense of being emotionally "healed."
- A clear perception and understanding of how negative emotion affects the energy body.
- A growing awareness of a profound connection between breath and emotion.
- A growing awareness that positive emotion is no different from radiant energy.

Stage 5 Exercise

Try doing a "light-weight" version of the "deep work" exercise from chapter 8. (Pay attention to the cautions noted.) Sustain this exercise for only twenty minutes. During the last ten to twenty minutes of your session, do a visualization exercise in which you visualize yourself healed of all emotional hurts, loving and radiating love and pleasure in all directions to everyone in the world. Do this while taking great pleasure in the process of your breath. When you are in this stage, you may on occasion wish to do the breathing exercise from chapter 6.

Stage 6: The Subtler Expressions of Life Energy

In this stage of the process, you begin to notice how life energy is continuous with even subtler levels of your life experience. Mental attitudes, expectations about the future, and intuitive capacities are all continuous with the life force we feel as energy in our body or as emotion. If we are to progress into greater subtlety, however, the grosser dimensions must be harmonious. Harmonious body and emotion are a necessary foundation for doing work at this stage.

Stage 6 Signs

- The ability to take responsibility for negative emotional states.
- Increased compassion for yourself and others.
- Increased mental clarity.
- A sense of yourself as continuous with, and not really separate from, the process of life itself.
- A direct sense of how you may help to create your own "luck."
- Keener and more confident intuitive judgment.

Stage 6 Exercise

Do the psychic sensitivity visualization exercise from chapter 9. Remember, however, that the physically based life energy and emotion must be in harmony before you can do this level of work with complete success.

III

This Subtle Science

Chapter 11

Lindemann's Advanced Work

In the process of working to heal himself using biocircuitry, Peter Lindemann developed not only a host of specific techniques, but also a theoretical framework for understanding the principles of biocircuitry. His experiments have convinced me that biocircuits are an effective medium for receiving detailed information about the whole body directly from its energy field and for communicating healing information to the body purely, directly, and effectively.

The Circuit Carries Information

Between 1976 and 1981, Lindemann explored a wide range of specific techniques. In some experiments he wired the biocircuit into other devices. "I found that when I wired the biocircuit to an orgone accumulator, for instance, my experience of the energy in circuit increased dramatically. This was useful and enjoyable, but it didn't relieve my symptoms." Other experiments included grounding the circuit and hooking it to copper spheres mounted on his roof. Lindemann placed a variety of substances in the circuit, extending the kinds of experiments done by Eeman, Maby, and Eric Powell. Some of these experiments produced beneficial results, but Lindemann still had not found an influence that "matched" and therefore eliminated his herpes symptoms.

Lindemann came to an important insight, however. He considered Eeman and Maby's drug circuits and Powell's "autonormaliser" and concluded, "The relaxation circuit must be able to carry detailed vibrational information." Lindemann theorized that the biocircuit carried not only the vibrational patterns of drugs or medicines placed in circuit, but also the unique complex vibrational imprint of the body-mind.

Once he became convinced that the energy running in the Eeman circuit contained a vast amount of information, he shifted his emphasis. Instead of merely increasing the quantity or quality of energy in the circuit, Lindemann wanted to "talk with" his energy body directly so he could discover and supply the healing information that would actually relieve his symptoms.

Lindemann's view of life energy as *conscious* is fundamental to these experiments. Eeman's work had established that the energy flowing in the biocircuit carries information. A well-established tenet within both Eastern and Western life-energy sciences is that the body *itself* is naturally intelligent. According to Lindemann's understanding, the life energy carries information consciously and *intelligently*, as our minds carry memories, not unconsciously and passively, as a data cable carries transmitted information between two computers. The life energy that flows in the biocircuit is a peripheral expression of the same intelligence that *is* our minds. It is a somatic and cellular, nonverbal, and nonlinear expression of the same intelligence with which you read these words.

Lindemann's "Electric Chair"

Eeman had performed a series of experiments involving radionics.* The practice of radionics is illegal in the United States,

* *The field of radionics was developed by Albert Abrams, a physician in San Francisco at the beginning of this century. The literature documenting a wide range of theories is voluminous; most sources are concerned with communicating and influencing the unique vibrational frequencies associated with the life field of every life form. Radionic theorists describe the human being as a vast system of energy resonant with a complex harmonic of wave forms. The radionic practitioner tunes into these frequencies and reads or transmits information. There are unique frequency rates for the different bodily organs, diseases, and medicines. (There are even different charts and systems of radionic rates.)*

because, from both a common-sense and mechanistic-scientific point of view, it doesn't do anything "real." Radionics sits with parapsychology on the border between science and magic. In fact, many people would describe it as a "scientific" format for the practice of magic, pure and simple. Most radionics practitioners use "black boxes" with many dials for tuning in "frequencies" or "rates."

In radionics, a vibrational "frequency" is assigned to almost anything conceivable, including diseases, injuries, body parts and organs, and homeopathic remedies. What makes radionics difficult to accept is that these radionic frequencies are not broadcast electromagnetically. Although in most radionics devices, the knobs are connected up in a logical wiring diagram, they are not hooked up to anything that logically affects anything else, and in some devices, the knobs are not even connected to anything!

Some of Eeman's drug experiments were tested by radionics practitioners. In these experiments, a radionics device was used to test individuals as they lay in the relaxation circuit with various drugs. Although the drugs were not identified, the radionics practitioner consistently succeeded in identifying the drugs' effects on the subjects' glands and organs.

Lindemann speculated that radionics might be a useful tool for reading his disease and providing a remedy. He obtained a radionics device and wired it directly into a reclining chair he had equipped with a copper biocircuit. His friends dubbed the resulting contraption "Peter's electric chair."

Lindemann dialed up the frequency for herpes simplex. When he lay in circuit with it, the device confirmed the presence of the same frequency in his system. When he lay in circuit with the radionics device and dialed up the frequency to treat himself for herpes, he immediately felt a powerful shift within his own energy field.

The results were dramatic and immediate. Lindemann was apparently successful in using the radionics device to "talk" with his energy field. His herpes symptoms diminished dramatically! Excited by this success, he did a series of experiments with the radionics device, obtaining equally dramatic results. Lindemann was impressed, although he was quick to tell me, "Science cannot account for why radionics should work at all. I found myself with a dramatic phenomenon begging for a theory to describe it."

Vibrational Grafting

Lindemann's radionics results were enigmatic, to say the least. He had achieved his most dramatic results with a modality that, he admitted, should do nothing at all! I can summarize his explanation as follows: "Many people agree that the power of the mind is central to healing. Malcolm Rae, among radionics theorists, has even called radionics devices 'thought simulators.' The radionics device is an objective vehicle through which abstract information can be symbolically expressed. In the biocircuit there is a subtle transfer of information that the radionics device responds to. The radionics device seems to be able to speak effectively through the biocircuit to the body's cellular intelligence." Although Lindemann was stretching my conceptions about the body and healing, what he said made sense. However, if I suspended my skepticism of radionics, other contradictions appeared.

According to radionics theory, it should not even be necessary to run the biocircuit through the radionics machine. At least in theory, the radionics device could work by means of a "witness" such as a lock of hair or a photograph. I asked Lindemann about this. He responded:

It's true [that] according to radionic principles, you don't need to hook up directly to the biocircuit. But I found it made a tremendous difference to hook up directly, particularly for treatment. The bottom line is intensity. The biocircuit is sim-

ply a very powerful medium for communicating information directly into the body's knowledge of how to build and heal itself, its "cellular intelligence." This is what my associate, Marty Martin, termed "vibrational grafting." When we did the original experiments, we called it a "vibrational graft" when we gave the cellular intelligence a piece of information that it incorporated fully. Observing the "grafting" process taught us a lot about the intelligence of the life force. If the vibration we were offering was wanted and needed by the body, the graft "took" easily, quickly, and completely. Precision and gentleness were the keys to this kind of success.

The power of the biocircuit as a medium for this communication is not limited to radionics, as Eeman's drug tests prove. You could introduce a very subtle vibratory set of instructions into a person's body via homeopathy, for example. But the body might not be willing to receive those instructions in that particular form, the oral ingestion of homeopathic tablets, even if they are the right set of instructions. When you put the instructions into the biocircuit, it's a different and very direct way of infusing the energy. The biocircuit directly "grafts" the new vibration right into the energy of the body.

Other delivery systems introduce vibrational influences, but none of them "graft" the influences as directly as the biocircuit. Using the biocircuit may make the crucial difference as to how deep or how well the vibration is incorporated. You can regulate the dose and effect, so that in many instances, one treatment is sufficient. What you're looking for is this total shift in the living energy field, which is the healing. After that, the symptoms go away in their own time. Using the biocircuit hooked into the radionic device, I've actually seen this shift, which is when the graft "takes." It happens right there, while they're in the chair. Sometimes this is dramatic.

"Vibrational grafting" does not depend on the use of radionics. "Any vibrational modality can be used with the biocircuit," Lindemann explained, "at least in theory. This could include drugs, herbs, homeopathy, cell salts, or even flower and gem essences." It is a matter of finding a common language through which you can communicate with the "cellular intelligence."

Lindemann found that radionics worked remarkably well, but other modalities might conceivably work better. What is of fundamental importance in this work is Lindemann's two-way communication with the energy body, and his understanding, codeveloped with his associate Marty Martin, of the "vibrational grafting" principle:

When you connect the body in a biocircuit, you set in motion a specific dynamic and promote a movement of life energy which wasn't there before. All natural therapies based on subtle energy, from homeopathy to acupuncture to radionics, are directed towards changing symptoms, towards producing movement. They don't presume to "heal" the patient. They assume that the body heals itself, and their treatment is always directed towards breaking up the "logjam" in that natural healing process, and catalyzing a change in which the natural living energy of the body is released to flow in the pattern of health. In the biocircuit, the life force is set in motion in a benign and healing fashion and so it creates a very good medium for ingesting the remedy.

"Empirically, the results I obtained were very persuasive," Lindemann concluded. His experiments with his "electric chair" yielded a wide range of dramatic successes, in terms of both analysis and treatment. "But I eventually discontinued this line of research because no matter how successful my results might be, it would probably never be legal for me to do anything practical with it in the United States."

Talking With DNA

Lindemann went on to describe vibrational grafting as a way of conversing directly with the body's DNA:

Marty Martin discovered that if for any reason the RNA function of the body is depressed, radionic treatments always failed to create an effective vibrational graft. By first stimulating the RNA with a specific treatment, all radionic treatments became effective. This was Martin's brilliant insight, which we interpreted in this way: all remedies are made in the body by the DNA! The radionic method is simply a way of talking to the DNA. But if the DNA can't get its message out into the cells through the RNA, the treatment won't work. The secret of successful vibrational grafting lies in this two-way conversation with what I call cellular intelligence, or living DNA.

Lindemann's theory, then, was that the biocircuit, connected to the radionics device, was a means for communicating more effectively with the intelligence of life:

Every substance has its own quality. Therefore it is always speaking to us. Our problem has been in the listening. I find the radionics device useful because it can separate the various qualities from one another so that they may be observed or strengthened individually. When one quality is separated out from all others, our analytical minds can "recognize it" distinct from the total soup of all qualities and then reintegrate it into its total understanding of health. In this way, a message which begins in the "cellular intelligence" can communicate its meaning to our verbal minds, and we can, in turn, influence it consciously. This process may also be reversed so that a conversation is set up. The total two-way process of communicating with the cellular intelligence of one's own body Marty and I called "talking with DNA."

Lindemann's use of the radionics device in connection with the biocircuit was closely tied to his view of health and healing itself:

The Intelligence of Life tells the chemicals of our bodies what

164

to do and not the reverse, as mechanistic science would have us think. DNA is the first physicalization of this Intelligence. The DNA controls each process and function in every cell of the body. It also controls all of the interactions of cells to form organs, systems of organs, and whole organisms. The amount of information your DNA organizes just to heal a simple cut would absolutely stagger your imagination.

As soon as an injury occurs, the DNA assesses the situation, determines what to do, and starts doing it. The body built itself from scratch in the first place and it uses this same set of instructions and procedures to repair itself no matter what the injury or dysfunction. It seems imperative to assume that the body not only can assess its own condition, but that it has its own predetermined methods to correct that condition down to the very last detail. The reason that everybody is not perfectly healthy is that the DNA's tasks have been inhibited by toxic deposits, unskillful choices, unresolved emotions, incorrect diet, and various other factors. The DNA knows how to correct these conditions, but it is up to us to stop creating them.

According to Lindemann's view of health and healing, then, the body always and only heals itself. All a human healer can do is facilitate that natural healing process:

All these vibrational modalities, including radionics, are simply a means for activating information resident in the DNA and precipitating it into physical motion and chemical activity. The trick is in discovering what the body has already decided to do, cooperating with that by helping to remove the root causes of imbalance, and activating the next step in the body's predetermined correction sequence. The remedy is not in the tuning or the homeopathic pills. Healing is a natural process and these vibrational therapies are all attempts to catalyze those natural processes, and accelerate what the body would normally do anyway.

Lindemann's Theoretical Model

There is no doubt that Lindemann is a very capable theoretician. Now I was interested in understanding my own basic biocircuit experience. I wanted to understand what happens when one individual lies in circuit without any external substances or devices wired in. I wanted to understand what principles are operative. Did Eeman's model of polarity fully explain the biocircuit phenomenon? Lindemann's explanations of the principles underlying the biocircuit's operation helped me to explain a variety of the phenomena I had observed.

I wanted to know whether Lindemann believed that the energy always moved in the same direction. He explained that the biocircuit creates a pathway whereby life force can move to another location:

Like water seeking its own level, the life force moves spontaneously to redistribute itself, correcting maldistribution and imbalance. The biocircuit is just an external structure through which that redistribution can occur. The body's energies frequently become habituated to a pattern of imbalance. The biocircuit enhances the energy's ability to be moved, changed, and repatterned. Thus, it reduces the tendency for energy to become discontinuous with the larger pattern.

Certainly there is a flow of energy, and I think it is a directional flow—a flow that moves from point A to point B, but the information does not necessarily always and only move in exactly the same direction.

Lindemann offered a metaphor: "The river may flow from the mountains to the sea, but the salmon can swim upstream."

Lindemann was apparently contradicting Eeman when he stated that the energy can move in *any* direction required for correcting imbalance. In fact, Lindemann stated directly that the flow does *not* always go in the same direction. When I considered Eeman's relaxation circuit, Lindemann's perspective on the direction of flow seemed problematic.

Eeman's polarity model elegantly explains the various relaxation circuits Eeman observed and distinguishes them clearly from the tension circuits he observed. Eeman theorized that the body was polarized from head to foot and right to left. The differential between the poles caused energy to flow through the circuit in a unique and consistent pattern. Eeman stated directly that the life energy *always* moves through the circuit *in the same direction*—from negative to positive. Further, he wrote that the energy flows "in a fixed and definite direction" from the left hand to the right.

When we discussed Lindemann's apparent contradiction of Eeman's theory, Lindemann offered a more comprehensive theoretical description of biocircuit operation. I found his comments enormously clarifying.

He pointed out that the biocircuit doesn't carry only raw energy containing information. The life energy itself carries a pattern of intelligence. When a person lies in the biocircuit, this energy redistributes itself. This is Eeman's model, and it is fundamental to the biocircuit phenomenon. *But the information carried by the energy is independently redistributed.* The most important factor in our experience of the biocircuit is not necessarily the movement of the energy itself; the movement of the information may be even more significant. Lindemann agrees with Eeman that the flow described by Eeman's polarity model is generally accurate as a description of the movement of the gross volume of life force. But according to Lindemann, it is not an accurate description of the movement of the information contained in that life force.

The transmission mode can be compared to that of the carrier frequency of a radio or television signal and the modulation of its signal into music or video images. The FM signal may be constant at 100.9 megahertz and 50,000 watts, but the music is constantly changing and moving. Lindemann says, "Life force may move from my left hand to the top of my spine, but information from all over my body may be communicated via that flow, and that movement of information may be the factor that most directly affects my ability to relax the accumulated tension in my neck."

Lindemann's Capacitance Discharge Model

In Lindemann's view, even the actual energy does not move smoothly in a single direction alone. "In the discharge of a capacitor," he explains, "the DC charge moves in one direction, but there are AC ripples within the DC charge, as well as high frequency ripples, which bounce back and forth or which move directly 'upstream' from the primary DC directional flow, and the flow of life force in the biocircuit behaves in the same fashion."

Lindemann's "capacitor" model of the biocircuit phenomenon is based on several different lines of reasoning and observation:

1. The human body behaves in a number of respects exactly like an electrical capacitor. Although life force and electricity are different kinds of energy, many similar principles govern their behavior. This is demonstrated by Nikola Tesla's experiments in which he passed hundreds of horsepower through his body via radio waves. This showed that, like a capacitor, the body is almost impervious to very high-frequency current.

2. The patterning and blocking of energy in the body is not just a matter of gross maldistribution of energy; it has to do with information as well.* Attitudes and memories are reflected and held by the body. These energy blockages contain information. When they release, the information releases with them. In fact, the release of

---

* *All the deep work described in chapter 8 concerns the connection between emotions and bodily "armoring."*

the information is likely to create the release of the blockages. Since the biocircuit helps to release these energy blocks, it seems obvious that it is redistributing information. But the blockages in the body occur differently in each individual. The information has to redistribute itself in a manner that is different in each individual case. Thus, the information must be moving in whatever direction is necessary to correct the unique imbalances of each particular individual.

3. It was Lindemann's own subjective impression that the biocircuit sets energy in motion throughout the body, enhancing the flow not just through the biocircuit, but everywhere. The energy, or at least information, moves in both directions in the biocircuit. My own subjective experience corroborates this statement. In fact, this observation has provoked me to raise these issues.

In my opinion, Eeman provided a basic model and Lindemann substantially refined it. Lindemann's capacitor model adds subtlety and sophistication to the original concept. Using it with Eeman's basic polarity model, we can clearly imagine not only the predictable flow of life force through the biocircuit, but the unpredictable flow of the information it carries.

Chapter 12

Eeman's Cooperative Circuitry

Eeman spent most of his life exploring the many exciting possibilities he discovered when he linked people together in what he called cooperative healing circuits. He felt the primary benefit of cooperative circuits was a dramatic boost in the quantity of circulating energy. Solo circuits do not increase the amount of life energy in the individual's biosystem; they only balance and harmonize the energy already present. But when many people lie in circuit, the quantity of energy circulating could be dramatically increased.

In addition, he felt that cooperative circuits might "dilute" the power of the imbalances or obstructions in individuals. Everyone's strengths could be pooled, thereby reducing the limitations of one individual's weakness and imbalance. Eeman conducted a healing practice, and he used cooperative circuits as a tool for bringing extra life energy to bear in the healing of his patients.

As his actual experimentation with cooperative circuits evolved, Eeman's most frequent distinct observation was that the individuals in circuit seemed to be sharing a single experience of the biocircuit. Every single individual in a cooperative circuit would feel rebalanced and relaxed at almost exactly the same time. The subjective sensation of the circuit's effects would also end simultaneously for everyone. If subjects fell asleep in circuit, they all awoke with uncanny simultaneity.

Cooperative circuits increased the subjective sense of the life energy in circuit, but they also presented new problems. Eeman made many of his most important theoretical discoveries while trying to work out the kinks in cooperative circuits.

The Left-Handed Problem

Occasionally, a particular cooperative circuit would produce effects that directly contradicted his most consistent results. Instead of warmth, relaxation, and a pleasant energy flow taking place between himself and the patient, an unbearable irritation would occur, making it impossible for either Eeman or his subject to continue in the cooperative circuit together. Eeman was well aware by now of the differences between tension and relaxation circuits. He knew the importance of wiring individuals together correctly in a cooperative relaxation circuit. Each time Eeman checked his wiring to make sure that he hadn't mistakenly wired a tension circuit between them. But in every case his wiring was correct.

In 1924, Eeman postulated that the reason for this was that certain individuals have inverted polarity.* To determine whether this inverted polarity had anything to do with sex or right- and left-handedness, or both, he devised the ingenious device he playfully called his "antisceptic battery." He used it to connect up to six people together in circuit and, unbe-

---

*For the sake of clarity, the authors have chosen this term. People with inverted polarity have opposite polarity charges throughout their bodies. As Eeman discovered, inverted polarity characterizes most left-handers. Their polarity charges are the complete inverse (as with a photographic negative) of the charges characterizing normal right-handers.

Reverse polarity, on the other hand, refers to people whose left hand and head have the same charge and whose right hand and sacrum have the same charge (as in a mirror image of the charges characterizing normal right-handers). For these people, a tension-circuit configuration produces a relaxation circuit. This is very rare.

Inverted polarity, which characterizes left-handers, needs to be accounted for only in cooperative circuits. When in solo circuits, left-handers can use all standard circuit configurations without modification.

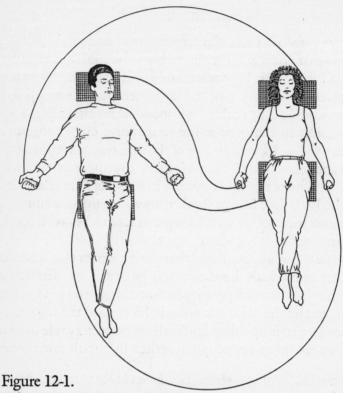

Figure 12-1.
The correct cooperative wiring between a right- and left-hander together in the circuit. See also Figures 12-3 and 12-4.

knownst to his subjects, alter the connections to eliminate certain subjects from the circuit without their knowledge.

One day, using his switching box, he connected two strong left-handers with two strong right-handers. As soon as they were connected in the standard wiring for a relaxation circuit, *all* the participants tensed up, their breathing became short and shallow, they became restless, and they complained of feeling cold. When Eeman changed the circuit so that right- and left-handers had their right hands and left hands connected respectively (see Figure 12-1), the subjects immediately and simul-

172

taneously heaved sighs of relief and their muscles relaxed. They slumped back, and became warm, peaceful, and comfortable.

Eeman then began a series of tests with left- and right-handers in cooperative circuits. By the end of the year he was able to conclude that the polarity of left-handers was the reverse of right-handers, *all the way up and down the nervous system*, irrespective of sex.* Thus, in solo circuits, such subjects would be wired no differently from right-handed individuals. (See Figure 12-2.) This polarity inversion would only become noticeable when they lay in circuit with right-handers.

But Eeman found other problems. The inclusion of a strong left-hander in a series of right-handers or vice versa produced a malaise that never appeared when right or left-handers were used exclusively. This malaise was even stronger and more widespread when the right- or left-hander occupied a middle position rather than the first or the last position in a series.

This phenomenon had nothing to do with the design of the circuit itself, because when Eeman reversed the circuit design, a tension circuit formed. Eeman's hypothesis was that "the human body [is] surrounded by an 'electro-magnetic' field of variable extent, strength, and polarity; and the polarity of left-handers being the reverse of right-handers, these two could not rest in parallel without the electro-magnetic fields interfering with each other and causing restlessness, tension, malaise"[1]. Eeman tested his hypothesis by resting the left-handers opposite to the right-handers (e.g., left-handers head-to-south; the right-handers head-to-north; see Figure 12-3). The malaise immediately disappeared!

Eeman then experimented with subjects in a square. His

* *"I occasionally met an 'ambidextrous' patient but soon convinced him that 'electro-magnetically' speaking, there was no such person. A few minutes spent alternately in each circuit showed that the so-called ambidextrous patient was electro-magnetically either right- or left-handed, and in the majority of cases, left-handed." Eeman,* Cooperative Healing, *p. 52.*

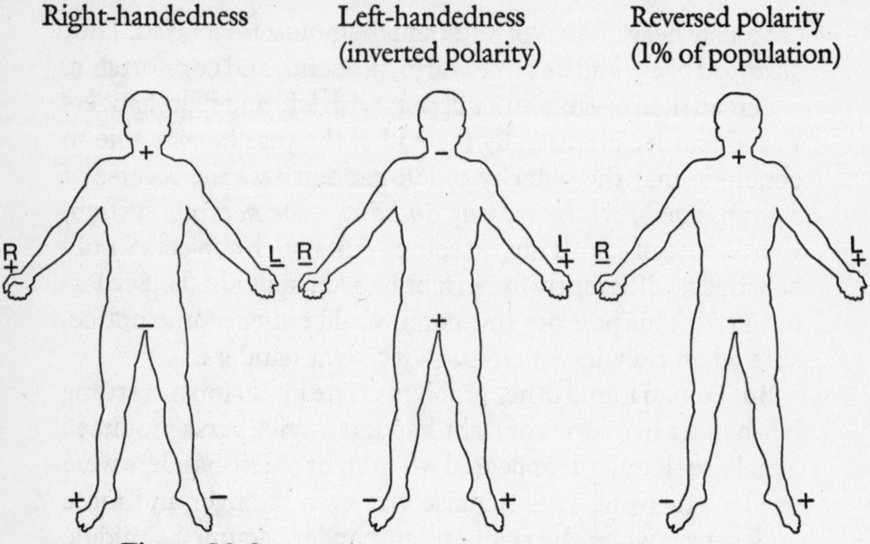

Right-handedness

Left-handedness
(inverted polarity)

Reversed polarity
(1% of population)

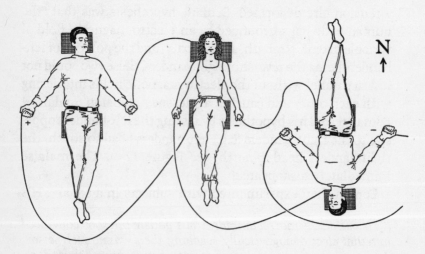

Figure 12-2.
The three types of polarity. This diagram illustrates the
difference between reversed polarity and inverted polarity.

Figure 12-3.
Three subjects in a relaxation circuit, left-hander head to south.

room was very small, and this configuration was easier to accomplish than a straight line. When he put his right-handers with their heads to the north and left-handers with their heads to the south, the malaise immediately disappeared. When he reversed the positions of left-hander and right-handed neighbors, making them respectively head to north and south, the malaise again disappeared! Again, the extent of this force field had to be taken into account.

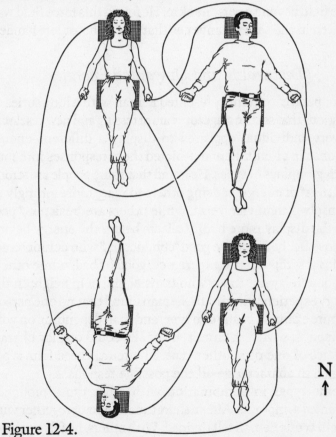

Figure 12-4.
Four subjects in a relaxation circuit in square, one right-hander head to south. Southeast subject is left-handed.

Thus, when not side by side, right- and left-handers in circuit had to rest head-to-feet, but same-handed subjects had to rest either head-to-head or feet-to-feet (Figure 12-4). By this simple test, Eeman found that this field reached all around the body to a width as great as four or five feet in some cases.

These experiments of Eeman's appear to validate the existence of an electromagnetic field extending well beyond the physical body. Eeman found he needed to take into account a force field beyond a person's skin. He found this force field was charged in the same manner as that of a right- or left-hander.

Disturbing and Unwanted Energies

Cooperative circuits presented Eeman with a long series of questions that set the stage for years of testing and new research.

Every individual appeared to display a different energy response in circuit. Eeman isolated these responses into four major groupings or types. He found that some people are strong "emitters" of energy, causing others to react more strongly to themselves than vice versa, while others are "resistors," people who display more bodily effects before the energy begins to move freely. Some are good "conductors," who demonstrate the least symptomatic experience, good or bad, while others are good "relayers," those who transfer and help heighten the energy experience in circuit. Eeman found that no one person is a pure example of any one type, and that, depending on who a person was with in circuit, he or she could display characteristics of one or another type. In circuit, these four types seemed to characterize all the possible responses.

Some types in combination with other types produced unwanted symptoms. After a short time in circuit together with certain types, Eeman felt drained. With others, he felt strained. Eeman found that he could affect the ease of the experience by varying the order in which he wired different types together. But he still wasn't satisfied.

He continued to work extensively with alternative types of circuitry for over twenty years, making an extremely concentrated effort from 1936 to 1940. With the aid of Cecil Maby, he considered thousands of cooperative circuits and in 1940 arrived at what he believed were the three optimal cooperative circuits. They minimized disturbing and unwanted energies most effectively by collecting the energy of everyone into a cooperative pool, and then redistributing the energy equally (see Figures 12-5, 12-6, and 12-7). Modeled on electrical wiring diagrams, these configurations were his "parallel" circuits.

Eeman devoted the bulk of his life work to cooperative circuits and cooperative healing, which he thought held great potential for healing. By the end of his life, he viewed the relaxation circuit mainly as a healing tool to be used in groups of two or more.

Treat Cooperative Circuits With Caution and Respect

Eeman felt that cooperative circuits had an advantage over laying on of hands by transferring energy via the whole of the sender's body, and therefore he considered them more powerful. Yet laying on of hands operates very differently than a cooperative circuit. In laying on of hands, the sender consciously and intentionally directs energy via the hands to specific areas of the receiver. In cooperative circuits, not only is healing energy transferred, but the entire energy pattern of each individual in circuit is indiscriminately mixed. Cooperative circuitry is passive; laying on of hands is a deliberate act. Dolores Krieger, in her book *The Therapeutic Touch*, notes, "I am quite convinced that the major expertise of the healer lies in the healer's ability to *direct* energies."[2] Shared circuitry certainly does not accomplish this discrimination.

Eeman was well aware that people sometimes received undesired physical symptoms in cooperative circuits. He spent

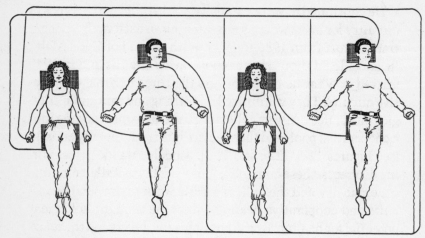

Figure 12-5.
Maby's Number 4.
Combination of parallelism and serialism. All right hands to all
left hands in parallelism. Each head to next spine in serialism.

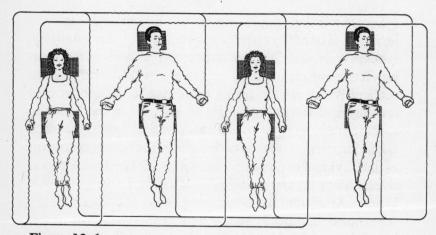

Figure 12-6.
Eeman's Number 1.
All head to all spine and all right to all left hands in pure parallelism.

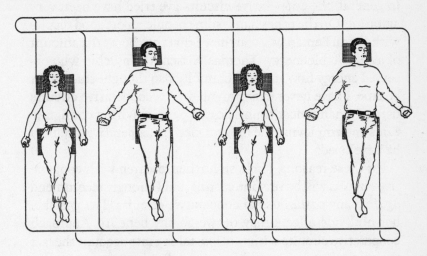

Figure 12-7.
Eeman's Number 2.
All heads to all left hands and all right
hands to all spines in pure parallelism.

years trying to create a system for cooperative circuitry that
would eliminate this problem. His best cooperative circuits
were parallel circuits. These employed the principle of a shared
energy pool. Still, he was never able to perfect his system and
totally eliminate unwanted and abnormal factors.

Anne Atkinson, a prominent radionics practitioner in
England, wrote to me of her association with Eeman and his
cooperative circuit: "Eeman knew I was using his method to
relax my patients but that I had given up group relaxation. I
found it could produce alarming results. I agree with Aubrey
Westlake when he says that Eeman's early demise was probably due to getting in circuit with others."

I have not had good experiences with cooperative circuits.
Once, while lying in a cooperative circuit with my husband
to help alleviate his headache, I soon had the headache too.

In general, the cooperative circuits I've tried have been very agitating. On the other hand, some people report good results with them. Eeman was convinced that they boost the amount of available bioenergy. Thomas Hirsch, the psychic who observed energy flow in the biocircuit, also thought this might be true. I have never experimented with cooperative circuits using Eeman's most sophisticated parallel wiring configurations and employing the full "science" of cooperative circuitry he developed.

For these reasons, I believe further research with cooperative circuits will be very interesting, but I strongly recommend *against* any *casual* use of cooperative circuits. The possible harmful side effects may outweigh any benefits. Approach cooperative circuits with caution, taking into account the fact that they mix energies indiscriminately. I suspect we may dis-

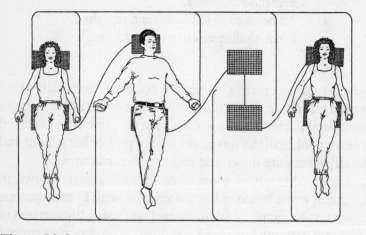

Figure 12-8.
Eeman's revised circuit Number 2.
When the Eeman optimal circuit is used, one person can leave without breaking the cooperative circuit.

cover valuable and safe uses for them and that research will yield risk-free cooperative techniques. Perhaps all side effects can be eliminated with only healthy energies pooled. Eeman felt sure this was possible. In my view, cooperative circuits still require—and deserve—more investigation.

If you do want to experiment with cooperative circuits, begin by reading *Cooperative Healing*. Study Eeman's three optimal cooperative circuit diagrams, as well as his instructions on combining left- and right-handers in circuit together. The simplest is Eeman's revised edition of circuit number 2 (see figure 12-8). This circuit was altered to account for the discovery of the optimal circuit. With this wiring diagram, it is possible for one person to leave without breaking the entire circuit.

I *can* freely recommend, as an alternative to cooperative circuits, combining laying on of hands with the use of the biocircuit, a technique I feel is extremely powerful. This technique calls for one or more people to perform laying on of hands while the recipient lies in circuit *by him- or herself* (see the exercise at the end of chapter 9 for details). This is the safest and easiest method for enjoying at least some of the advantages of a cooperative circuit.

Notes

1. Eeman, *Cooperative Healing*, p. 63.
2. Krieger, *The Therapeutic Touch*, p. 56.

Chapter 13

What's Next?

What's next in the field of biocircuitry? What technological innovations are contemplated? What is Lindemann planning? What research directions promise the most interesting results?

Stretching the Boundaries of Awareness

Biocircuits are not the only tool for contacting deep levels of body, emotion, mind, and psyche. Drugs, primal therapy, and hypnosis, for example, all produce more dramatic effects. *The unique value of biocircuits is that they empower such exploration without violently displacing our ordinary consciousness.* They are tools for stretching the boundaries of our awareness.

Biocircuits are not the quickest way to enter supernormal states of consciousness (or deep perinatal emotional levels or creative hypnagogic states). But if you want to be able to enter such states on your own, you'll have to learn the territory between here and there. Otherwise, you are likely to find the trip confusing and give up or get lost. Biocircuits are a uniquely useful tool for stretching the boundaries of our conscious experience and exploring that territory. They provide a boost, but they leave us conscious and relaxed and in full possession of our intentional faculties. Systematic exploration of these potentials is in my view *the* most exciting area for new research in biocircuitry.

Lindemann's "Supercircuit"

Peter Lindemann has lately begun experimenting, in both

copper and silk, with a six-point circuit that makes *every possible* cross-polar connection (see Figure 13-1). This is a combination of every possible relaxation circuit using the hands, feet, and top and bottom of the spine. I have tried this circuit, and its subjective effects are very strong.

In considering the difference between Eeman's general and optimal circuits, Lindemann came to feel that additional biocircuit connections added to the momentum of the energy flow. He extended this principle to its logical conclusion in designing this "supercircuit." With this design, the energy momentum is greatest, and the energy has the greatest number of choices as to where it will flow in order to redistribute itself for dynamic balance.

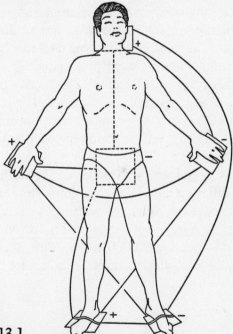

Figure 13-1.
Lindemann's "supercircuit."
Every possible cross-polar connection is made to produce
a very powerful effect.

Lindemann's initial feeling is that the supercircuit may provide a more profound balancing effect than any of the other biocircuit configurations he has considered. However, some early users have been disturbed by the strength of the circuit's influence. The first phase of the biocircuit experience intensifies imbalances, which then resolve into a profound harmony. For some individuals, the first phase in this circuit has been "too much." Lindemann considers the supercircuit still in the "experimental" phase.

Alternate Materials

An important opportunity for innovation is the construction of biocircuits from new and different materials, many of which would theoretically serve as benign conductors for life energy. Among the metals, Lindemann feels that carbon, stainless steel, and gold seem most promising. Glass and water would, in theory, provide excellent conductive materials for a biocircuit. (Water especially, is an extremely clean and quick conductor of life energy.) However, both glass and water present obvious, amusing, and imposing engineering and construction problems!

An interesting and potentially significant possibility involves combining different metals, such as copper and zinc, in a single biocircuit device. Japanese acupuncture techniques, including some that have been associated with Manaka's "ion pumping cords" (see Appendix I), use the differentials between needles made of different metals to create therapeutic influences.

Vibrational Grafting

Numerous researchers have confirmed the value of substance circuits. Lindemann's advanced "vibrational grafting" work suggests that effective vibrational influences can be extremely subtle. Therefore, at least in theory, vibrational grafting can address a broad spectrum of imbalances in the human energy field. One of the obvious important areas for new research is the systematic application of this technology to various specific energy imbalances.

Of particular interest are substance circuits with a universally beneficial effect. Some stresses to health operate upon all human beings. For instance, disease patterns have been correlated with sunspot activity. Chemical and electromagnetic pollution may be important contributors to various viral and immune disorders. Many other such influences have been suggested. Specific substances or vibrational influences placed in the biocircuit may be able to strengthen the biofield's resistance to such stresses. This is an opportunity for important new research. It is important to identify influences that provide universal benefits and to develop or refine procedures for conducting such vibrational grafting.

Cooperative Circuits

An extremely exciting area for new biocircuit research involves using cooperative circuits with healthy subjects for experiments with positive group consciousness. As suggested in the preceding chapter, such work should be done cautiously. Eeman's years of experiments with cooperative healing involved linking sick patients with healthy people in a large biocircuit for healing purposes. I have cautioned against casually experimenting with the indiscriminate sharing of diseased energy patterns via cooperative circuits.

But cooperative circuits do not have to be used remedially. They can be used by groups of healthy people.* According to Eeman, cooperative circuits powerfully increase the energy

---

* Even healthy people using cooperative circuits for positive purposes should treat them with respect, and use them only after consulting Eeman's book Cooperative Healing.

experience in the biocircuit. He used them for healing purposes, but he also found their use highly pleasurable. Cooperative circuits might be particularly interesting when linking people who share a positive emotional connection as well as a common intention, especially if they share an intuitive and attitudinal foundation. I am aware of such people experimenting with group meditations and visualizations and other practices, thereby creating and sharing an experience of "group consciousness." Biocircuits offer a very direct and powerful way to magnify such practices.

In addition, the healthful use of cooperative circuits may have a dynamic power on a larger scale. Many people, using techniques ranging from meditation to visualization to prayer, attempt to influence the "mind of the planet" towards positive outcomes. Rupert Sheldrake's "morphogenetic field" theory has even suggested a scientific explanation for a mechanism by which such practices might actually produce their desired effects.

When people link their life energies together in a group biocircuit, in theory they should create a supersystem of conscious energy, a powerful broadcast antenna for their conscious intention. By lying in a cooperative circuit, they should become much more powerful than they would be outside the biocircuit. Although this premise is theoretical and awaits experimental verification, it points in a very interesting direction for future biocircuit work.

Appendices

Appendix I

The Japan Connection

During World War II, supplies ran low at the military hospital where Dr. Yoshio Manaka cared for a ward crowded with wounded soldiers, many suffering severe burns. Dr. Manaka was a surgeon trained in Japanese acupuncture. With no ointments available, Dr. Manaka had wrapped tin over the burns to neutralize the ionic discharge from the wounds. Noticing some improvement, he experimented by attaching a wire to the tin and connecting it with an unburned area on the other side of the body (for example, burned left arm to unburned right arm). In response to this simple method alone, the burns healed in record time. With no knowledge of Eeman or his experiments, Manaka had stumbled upon an effective biocircuit!

Although Manaka's work does not stand in the biocircuit tradition documented in this book, it has major significance, because it independently corroborates the biocircuit phenomenon. It also focuses on important healing effects that are produced by external connections between points on the body—and involving no energy source other than the body itself. Manaka has written that he feels his biocircuit experiments demonstrate that Chi—life energy—exists.

Dr. Manaka, however, did not theorize a complete circuit of Chi. Instead, he described the phenomenon entirely in terms of ions flowing through his connecting wire. Burn wounds produce an abundance of positive ions, and Dr. Manaka conceived his original experiments as a means of neutralizing them, first by laying conductive metal against the wound, and later by conducting this charge away from the wound via the connector wires.

Manaka continued his experiments after the war. He theorized that a tiny electrical current moved along the wire, and that the success of the arrangement depended upon the flow moving in the right direction. Accordingly, he designed several mechanisms for controlling that ion flow. He placed subjects on an insulated table and attached a Vandergraf generator to one part of their bodies. (A Vandergraf generator can create a powerful positive or negative static charge.) Then he attached the charged part of the body to an uncharged part of the body with a copper or steel wire. In this way, he was able to induce a small current and control the direction of the ionic flow. This part of Manaka's work parallels work done by Dr. Robert O. Becker on the effects of tiny electrical currents in the healing of bone tissue.

Manaka proved himself a masterful theoretician and an innovative genius. His experiments combined biocircuit work with advances in knowledge about acupuncture meridians. Much of his research deals with theories about interlocking meridian systems and advanced therapeutic approaches within Japanese acupuncture.

Manaka eventually began connecting acupuncture needles placed in particular acupuncture points via copper wires into which he inserted high-quality, low-resistance germanium diodes. He introduced no external electricity but knew that the body's own electromagnetic field would stimulate a tiny current in the wire. In this way, he controlled the directionality of the ionic flow along the wires. This technique proved to be extremely effective, and a sophisticated therapeutic theory for using this technique has developed. Following Manaka, other Japanese acupuncturists have developed new applications for this biocircuitry. "Ion pumping cords" have made it possible to achieve therapeutic results that were unattainable when the wire was connected without the diode.

Dr. Manaka's "ion pumping cords" have been recognized as an important contribution to contemporary Japanese acupuncture. Today they are used to connect both needles and supercutaneous electrodes. Owing to Manaka's research, these biocircuits have been used on thousands of acupuncture patients and have probably become the most widely used biocircuits in the world to date. Manaka himself is among the most famous and highly respected acupuncturists in Japan, and he is particularly famous for his work in anesthesia and pain relief. Now, at age seventy-seven, he heads a hospital in Odawara, near Tokyo.

Dr. Manaka and his students explain the phenomenon of his biocircuits in purely electrical terms. Although the magnetic field surrounding the wires has been estimated at less than .5 gauss, Steven Birch, of the New England School of Acupuncture, has stated that the current cannot be accurately measured. The current is so minute that any measurement device alters the current flow significantly. Nonetheless, acupuncture theory asserts that the wire itself cannot conduct anything other than electricity. Most contemporary acupuncturists believe that the current that flows through the wire is converted into Chi when it hits the body surface.

Perhaps Manaka is right, and his wires conduct only ions: electrical energy. At first Eeman also believed that his relaxation circuit conducted subtle electricity. Only late in his life, after he had observed the operation of the silk circuit, did he conclude that another, nonelectromagnetic, energy flowed through the wires. The distinction between electricity and life energy may not be an absolute one. In fact, even if the flow through the wires is exclusively electrical, the wire is only half the complete circuit, and the other half flows through the living body. I believe that the electricity flowing through the body coincides with what we call life energy.

It seems possible to me that life energy may flow through Manaka's wires. Wilhelm Reich observed that flowing orgone energy can register on instruments measuring electricity. Is it not conceivable that life energy flowing through copper wires expresses a tiny electrical current? Perhaps the biocircuit flow includes a whole spectrum of energies, including electrical, etheric, and astral energies.

190

The efficacy of silk biocircuits certainly *suggests* that non-electrical energy may flow in Manaka's ion pumping cords. Whether this is true or not, Manaka's work demonstrates that "when you polarize energy on the surface of the body, profound and significant healing effects can occur."[1]

Notes

1. Steven Birch, the New England School of Acupuncture, in a telephone conversation with the author.

Appendix II

Additional Biocircuit Configurations and Their Uses

More Circuits

The Tension Circuit and Its Uses

Tension circuits are mainly used to reverse the effects of an overlong period spent in the relaxation circuit. If you fall asleep in circuit and wake up feeling imbalanced and enervated, a few minutes in a tension circuit will quickly correct this.

Another use for the tension circuit is to "refocus" a very fatigued and enervated body. A short time in the circuit (and you must become sensitive to exactly how long) will restore vitality. If you feel you have spent too long in this circuit, your energy imbalance can be corrected by a short time in the relaxation circuit.

There are three tension circuits. The first is an adaptation of either of Eeman's circuits. Simply reverse the handles, connecting the right hand to the head and the left hand to the base of the spine (Figure A-1).*

The second tension circuit is adapted from Lindemann's centrally symmetrical circuit. Since the Lindemann circuit is a "universal relaxation circuit," his tension circuit is universal as well. That is, it will have the same effect on everyone. To make this circuit, simply connect each hand to the same-side foot. Thus, the right hand is connected to the right foot, the left hand is connected to the left foot, and the head to spine connection is left intact (Figure A-2).

This last tension circuit is unique among the three, because

* *For those rare individuals with reverse polarity, a tension circuit will resemble the relaxation circuit.*

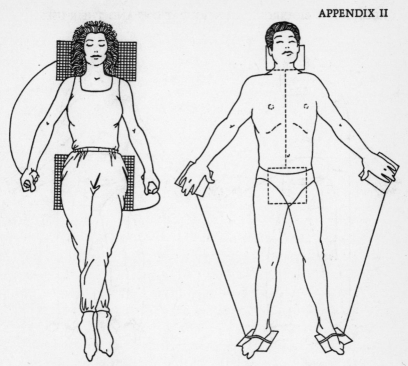

Figure A-1. (left)
The Eeman tension circuit. Simply reverse the handles of a
standard relaxation circuit to create this tension circuit.
Figure A-2. (right)
Lindemann's universal tension circuit.

it includes the whole body but is not a centrally symmetrical
circuit. It is illustrated in Figure A-3. It is the reverse of the relaxation circuit discussed below.

A Whole-Body Left-to-Right Circuit

This circuit balances the body left to right, yet it includes
the feet. Figure A-4 shows that the base of the spine is connected
to the right foot, while the head is connected to the left foot.
The hands are connected to each other. This circuit requires
one extra-long connection.

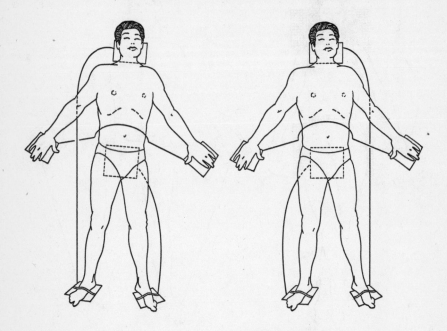

Figure A-3.
A whole-body left-to-right
tension circuit.

Figure A-4.
A whole-body left-to-right
relaxation circuit.

Another Centrally Symmetrical Circuit

This is another excellent circuit that balances both left to right and vertically. It can be performed as in Figure A-5, or, as an alternative to using pads on each foot, the legs can be bent at the knee and the feet placed sole to sole. This circuit is very relaxing, although there is little circular movement of the life energy.

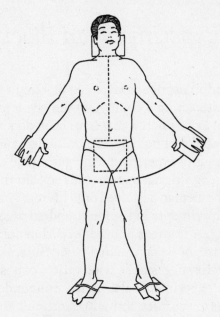

Figure A-5.
An alternative universal
centrally symmetrical circuit. The feet can also be
placed sole to sole, knees
bent, instead of on the
foot pads.

Appendix III

Other Experiments in Biocircuitry

This appendix describes a few other biocircuit experiments I find most interesting. I could not even begin to recount all of the diverse experiments that have been done with biocircuits and related technologies. Peter Lindemann alone conducted hundreds of experiments increasing the energy in the circuit and using alternative materials and alternative circuit configurations. Eeman described only his most important and successful experiments in the four hundred pages of *Cooperative Healing*. A number of other experimenters have used devices that might be considered biocircuits.

This appendix suggests the wide variety of possible experiments. These experiments also increase our understanding of the properties of the force active in the circuit and offer extra guidelines for our own work with biocircuits.

Orgone Accumulators and the Biocircuit

Orgone accumulators were invented in the 1940s by Wilhelm Reich. Reich found that by alternating layers of organic materials and metals, he was able to construct a device that accumulated orgone energy. The organic material, such as wool or cotton, attracts and absorbs the energy while the metallic material attracts and repels it again rapidly. The organic material draws the energy from the atmosphere and transfers it to the metal on the inside. The metal in turn repels this energy both toward the inside of the accumulator and back to the cotton. Therefore, the movement of energy into the accumulator is free, while the movement back into the atmosphere is prevented. Thus, the greatest accumulated surplus of energy resides inside the box. This energy Reich called "orgone" energy.

By sitting in an orgone box, wrapping oneself in an orgone blanket, or even applying orgone energy locally by use of a flexible tube running through an accumulator, an organism is energized. And indeed, Reich did many experiments using orgone energy therapeutically, compiling notes on its various characteristics and properties.

Peter Lindemann's research with orgone accumulators and biocircuits is quite extensive. Lindemann started with the supposition that the energy in an orgone accumulator and the energy in a biocircuit were related and possibly identical. His very first system using Reich's principles was composed of a pair of six-inch-in-diameter copper plates for pads covered with cotton and steel wool, part of the formula for an orgone accumulator. His intention was to try to increase the amount of life force moving in the circuit. This experiment didn't produce the results he was hoping for.

Lindemann conducted a wide variety of experiments with orgone energy and biocircuits, including wrapping himself in an orgone blanket while lying on the screens (this did increase the total energy in the circuit). But his most successful orgone experiment ran the circuit through the center of an accumulator.

Lindemann built a small orgone accumulator of a radical new design. He allowed the energy in the biocircuit to pass directly onto the core of the accumulator, where the orgone was accumulating to the highest degree. He explains that out of all his experiments, this was the most effective in amplifying and strengthening the effect of the biocircuit. "When the circuit was completed across the core of the accumulator, it felt like twice as much energy was moving in the circuit."

Magnets

Bob Nelson of Rex Research in Berkeley describes a technique he regularly uses to increase total circuit energy. By substituting magnets with homogeneous poles (round magnets) for the handles on a copper biocircuit, Nelson claims he is able to increase the total energy effect.

In another experiment with magnets that is claimed to increase the energy in the circuit, the individual, while lying in circuit, holds a carbon rod in one hand and a small horseshoe magnet in the other. Depending on which hand is used for the carbon rod, the subject may find that his or her energy increases or decreases. Borderland Sciences Research Foundation has found that the hardened carbon seems to energize the nervous system, while the magnet amplifies or enhances this effect. The firm is marketing a device using these principles called the "Vitic," which is claimed to have a stimulating effect. Many users report feeling a pulsing sensation in their hands as well.

Unique Materials

Dr. Manaka's "ion pumping cords" can be used in place of copper wire between each handle and screen. These wires are currently used with acupuncture needles in Japan to help induce the energy flow in the meridians. They are simple in design: copper wires with a germanium diode that permits ions to flow in one direction only. I suspect the diode also controls the directional flow of life energy. Therefore, it is important that they be hooked up correctly. Users report that these cords help speed up the energy, producing immediate results from the circuit. Ion pumping cords can be purchased through local Oriental medical supply companies.

Crystals

Many people claim they can increase the sense of the energy flowing in the circuit by holding a crystal in each hand while relaxing in the biocircuit. Try using crystals that have a point at one end. The pointed end indicates the direction in which the energy flows. Experiment with how you hold the crystal in your hand and see if it makes a difference. For right-handers, the direction of energy flow in an Eeman optimal circuit is from left to right. Therefore, hold the crystal in your left hand pointed in toward your arm; the crystal in your right hand points out. Left-handers should reverse this.

One user told me he heightened the energy effects significantly by lying on the floor with large crystals surrounding and pointing toward his body. He used five crystals, one at each foot and hand and one near his head. Other configurations have been used with success also. Crystals can be powerful. Be sensitive and careful: they can be used correctly or incorrectly, and when used improperly, the effects are not benign.

The Body's Phantom Energy Field

People with an amputated leg often say they can still feel its presence. They feel itches, cramps, or tingling, or other familiar sensations in the missing leg. Psychics say they can actually see phantom limbs still attached to the body. This is explained by modern medicine as old sensory patterns in the brain, traces of memory of the missing limb that persist in those parts of the nervous system concerned with its movements or sensations.

Eeman did some provocative experiments with people missing limbs. He placed copper mesh bands around the subjects' knees and existing foot (if there was one) and glass bottles with copper mesh bands wrapped around them where the foot or feet might have been. The subject then held a copper handle lightly in each hand. Each handle and mesh band had six wires attached to it. These were connected to a switching box. By alternating the connections between the missing foot (or feet) and various other points without the subject's knowledge, the subject was able to tell if his missing leg(s) had been included in the circuit. The phantom leg would feel warm all the way down to the phantom foot. The subject could also distinguish whether the circuit had been made between his hands and real knees or between his hands and foot bottles. Then Eeman tried placing a drug in solution through the circuit at the subjects' "assumed" feet. The subjects responded appropriately to the drug.

Because he had only a limited number of patients with whom he could perform such experiments, Eeman wasn't able to do enough trials to formulate definitive conclusions. Yet these experiments suggest that this invisible field remains intact even after physical parts are amputated.

Cayce's Impedance and Wet-Cell Devices

The impedance device (sometimes called the radial-active device) and the wet-cell device were first channeled by Edgar Cayce in 1925 in response to questions about specific illnesses. While the impedance device is used mostly for basic body balancing, the wet-cell device has more specific applications and is generally recommended for serious conditions involving inactive organs and/or glands that need stimulation. The wet cell sends a very low form of electrical vibration designed primarily to affect the central nervous system. The wet cell operates under the assumption that the central nervous system needs a small amount of electricity to relay healing impulses. Since the wet cell is more elaborate and is used for specific diseases, for the purposes of researching this book I concentrated on the impedance device, one of which I built and have used.

The impedance device first came to my attention because it is specifically recommended for nervous system disorders. It supposedly affects the circulatory system, causing increased circulation to and through the extremities. This action aids the blood, lymph, and nerves and induces sleep or relaxation.

It is not a battery and has no electrical charge. The theory behind the device is that the circulatory system operates principally in conjunction with the body's magnetic field. Cayce claimed that the device itself forms a "magnetic field" or becomes a magnet with use. In other words, the device itself is not magnetic, but our own bodies magnetize impedance devices attached to them. This induced magnetic field resonates with the body's own field, bringing the different bodily frequencies at specific localized points within the normal range of functioning.[1] This process has been compared to the balancing effect of acupuncture, but without the needles. Professor William Tiller of Stanford University explains the workings of the device: "The appliance sets up an oscillatory energy pattern in the body causing current flow out of some acupuncture points and current input into others. . . . This continual flow, this gentle oscillation, is bringing about a balancing of the energy circuits . . . an equalization process, the taking from one meridian and giving to another."[2]

The impedance device is a type of capacitor. The device consists of two thin pieces of glass surrounded by two pieces of carbon steel and four pieces of carbon blocks. This entire bundle is taped together, put into a container filled with charcoal, and then sealed. Two electrodes, one copper and one nickel, run from the device to one's body.

There is a systematic means of attaching these plates to the body based on body polarity. Each day, for four consecutive days, the plates are attached to different poles of the body until, after the fourth day, the entire system is rejuvenated. This procedure can then be repeated several times. Thus, the device works by repolarizing the system. ("Circulation moves in a figure 8. The first extremity attached becomes a positive pole. Energy is discharged in the opposite pole. The appliance becomes a magnet.")[3] After some extensive reading into the device, I felt that in calling this a "circulatory device," Cayce meant it affected the circulation of the energy field (which in turn would affect the gross circulation of the blood). Obviously, it is the energy that moves in a figure 8, not the blood circulation.

An interesting addition to the impedance device and the wet cell is the solution jar. Cayce specified the use of medicinal solutions for many ailments. The solution jar was simply a five- or six-ounce jar through which the circuit ran. Depending upon the ailment being treated, many different solutions were advised, including silver nitrate, gold chloride, camphor, and tincture of iodine.

Cayce's explanation of how the solutions affect the body without ingestion is that a low electrical charge is produced chemically that carries the vibrations from the solutions into the body. Tiller concurs:

When the current flows through the solution, if there is good coupling between these, then the energy stream that is passing into the excitation circuit of the body picks up the vibratory quality of whatever is in the solution jar and it moves this quality into the body along the circuit paths of the various currents. If there are centers within the body, or molecules which absorb and radiate in the frequency band of these vibratory qualities, then the elements of that area will just absorb the resonant wave patterns. The elements, molecules or glands will gain, in fact, the value that they would have gained from the minerals themselves. Thus, the function of the solution jar is to serve as a current modulation device.[4]

This theory agrees with Eeman's completely. Cayce, Tiller, and Eeman all agree that the current (or carrier wave) is modulated and that this modification resonates with similar vibratory elements in the body. Whatever explanation is correct, it is interesting that Cayce recommends vibrational grafting as a viable means of healing the system.

Cayce said that no symptoms would be felt during a session with the impedance device. In fact, he noted it might take several weeks to feel any subjective changes. The only noticeable effect during use might be a feeling of sleepiness. Thus, the device seems not to sensitize the user to the energy body but simply to bring it into harmonious resonance after several uses. The impedance device is compared in A.R.E. (Cayce's organization) literature to the Eeman biocircuit. "It may be stated that the nature of [Eeman's] experiments and their effects are so similar to the use of the Impedance Appliance that it seems a common theory may be involved . . . [*Cooperative Healing*] is suggested as parallel reading for anyone interested in the Impedance or Wet-Cell Appliances."[5]

Notes

1. Special thanks to Phil Thomas, who clarified the workings of the impedance device in a letter to the author dated July 14, 1987.
2. Tiller, "Energy Fields and the Human Body, Part II," p. 14.
3. Button, *The Radial-Active Device*.
4. Tiller, "Energy Fields and the Human Body, Part II," p. 15.
5. Cayce, *Two Electrical Appliances Described in the Edgar Cayce Readings*, p. 16.

Bibliography

Abrams, A. *New Concepts in Diagnosis and Treatment.* San Francisco: Philopolis Press, 1916.

Amber, R. *Color Therapy.* New York: Aurora, 1983.

Armstrong, J. W. *The Water of Life: A Treatise on Urine Therapy.* Essex, England: Health Science Press, 1971.

Beck, R. "Mood Modification with ELF Magnetic Fields: A Preliminary Exploration," *Archaeus 4,* 1986: 47–53.

Becker, R. "The Direct Current Control System: A Link Between Environment and Organism," *New York State Journal of Medicine* (April 15, 1962): 1169–1176.

Becker, R., and G. Selden. *Body Electric: Electromagnetism and the Foundation of Life.* New York: Morrow, 1985.

Bhattacharyya, Dr. B. *Magnet Dowsing or the Magnet Study of Life.* Calcutta: Firma KLM Private Limited, 1981.

Birren, F. *Color and Human Response.* New York: Van Nostrand Reinhold, 1978.

Buranell, V. *The Wizard From Vienna: Franz Anton Mesmer.* New York: Coward, McCann, and Geoghegan, 1975.

Burke, A. *Magnetic Therapy.* Marina del Rey, Calif.: De Vorss, 1980.

Burr, H. S. *Blueprint for Immortality: The Electric Patterns of Life.* London: Neville Spearman, 1972.

Butler, W. E. *How to Read the Aura, Practice Psychometry, Telepathy and Clairvoyance.* New York: Warner/Destiny, 1978.

Button, D. *The Wet Cell Battery Device. All That Edgar Cayce Said About It.* Self-published. No date.

———. *The Medicinal Solution Inducing Device. Metallic-Mineral-Vegetable for Use With the Wet Cell or Radial-Active Devices. All That Edgar Cayce Said About It.* Self-published. No date.

_____ . *The Radial-Active Device. All That Edgar Cayce Said About It.* Self-published. No date.

_____ . *The Plate Disk Electrode Attachment System for the Wet Cell and Radial-Active Devices. All That Edgar Cayce Said About Them.* Self-published. No date.

Cater, J. *The Awesome Life Force: The Hermetic Laws of the Universe as Applied to All Phenomena.* Mokelumne Hill, Calif.: Health Research, 1982.

Cayce, E. *Two Electrical Appliances Described in the Edgar Cayce Readings.* Virginia Beach: Association for Research and Enlightenment, 1965.

Cornillier, P. *The Prediction of the Future: A New Experimental Theory.* Translated from the French by L. E. Eeman. London: Partner Press, 1935.

Cotton, H. D. *Relax Your Way to Health.* London: Health for All Publishing, 1954.

Crile, G. *The Bipolar Theory of Living Processes.* New York: Macmillan, 1926.

_____ . *The Phenomena of Life: A Radio-Electrical Interpretation.* New York: Norton, 1936.

Da Free John. *Conscious Exercise and The Transcendental Sun.* Clearlake, Calif.: The Dawn Horse Press, 1977.

_____ . *The Eating Gorilla Comes in Peace. The Transcendental Principle of Life Applied to Diet and the Regenerative Discipline of True Health.* Middletown, Calif.: The Dawn Horse Press, 1979.

_____ . *The Illusion of Relatedness: Essays on True and Free Renunciation and the Radical Transcendence of Conditional Existence.* San Rafael, Calif.: The Dawn Horse Press, 1986.

_____ . *The Transmission of Doubt. Talks and Essays on the Transcendence of Scientific Materialism Through Radical Understanding.* San Rafael, Calif.: The Dawn Horse Press, 1984.

Davis, A., and A. K. Bhattacharya. *Magnet and Magnetic Fields.* Calcutta: Mukhopadhyay, 1970.

de la Warr, G., and D. Baker. *Biomagnetism.* Oxford: de la Warr Laboratories, 1967.

Drown, R. *The Theory and Technique of the Drown Homo-Vibra Ray.* Garberville, Calif.: Borderland Sciences Research Foundation (reprint of Hatchard & Co. Publication, London, 1939).

Eden, J. *Animal Magnetism and the Life Energy.* New York: Exposition Press, 1974.

Eeman, L. E. "Cooperative Healing." Garberville, Calif.: Borderland Sciences Research Foundation. (This is a small pamphlet of excerpts from Eeman's original 1947 edition by Frederick Muller.)

_____ . *Cooperative Healing.* Mokelumne Hill, Calif.: Health Research, 1987. (This is a reprint of the 1947 edition and is the only edition currently in print.)

_____ . *Cooperative Healing.* London: Frederick Muller, Ltd., 1947.

_____ . *Cooperative Healing and Reactions of the Human Body to the Frequencies of Drugs and Other Substances Placed in Series in the Relaxation Circuit: A Paper Read Before the British Society of Dowsers on Wednesday, the 13th October, 1943.* London: Author-Partner Press, 1943.

_____ . *Cooperative Healing. Retrospect and Forecast. A Paper Read Before the British Society of Dowsers on Wednesday, the 11th June, 1947.* London: Author-Partner Press, 1947.

_____ . "Creative Faith. The Ascending Series From Unbelief Through Disbelief, Doubt, Belief, and Faith to Wholeness of the Individual and of the Race." Reprinted from *The Journal of the British Society of Dowsers* (June 1952), No. 76.

_____ . *How Do You Sleep? The Basis of Good Health.* London: Author-Partner Press, 1939.

_____. "Interim Report After Thirty-five Years of Research. A Lecture Delivered to the British Society of Dowsers After the Annual General Meeting Held on October 20th, 1954." Reprinted from *Radio-Perception* (December 1954), Vol. XII, No. 86.

_____. "Psycho-Physical Effects of Conducted Radionic Emissions From Drugs and Bloods," *Proceedings of the Scientific and Technical Congress of Radionics and Radiesthesia.* London: May 16–18, 1950: 149–159.

_____. *Self and Superman.* London: Author-Partner Press, 1930.

_____. *The Subconscious Made Conscious.* London: Simpkin Marshall, 1926.

_____. *Technique of Conscious Evolution.* Essex: C. W. Daniel, 1956.

Elkin, A. P. *Aboriginal Men of High Degree.* St. Lucia: University of Queensland, 1977.

Gallert, M. *New Light on Therapeutic Energies.* London: James Clarke, 1966.

Gallimore, J. G. *Handbook of Unusual Energies. Volumes 1, 2, 3.* Mokelumne Hill, Calif.: Health Research, Vol. 1 (1976); Vol. 2, 3 (1977).

Galvani, L. *Commentary on the Effect of Electricity on Muscular Motion—A Translation of Luigi Galvani's De Viribus Electricitatis in Motu Musculari Commentarius.* Cambridge, Mass.: E. Licht, 1953.

Gerber, R., M.D. *Vibrational Medicine: New Choices for Healing Ourselves.* Santa Fe, N.M.: Bear, 1988.

Gimbel, T. *Healing Through Color.* Essex: C. W. Daniel, 1985.

Green, E., and A. Green. *Beyond Biofeedback.* Delacorte Press/Seymour Lawrence, 1977.

Grof, S. *The Adventure of Self-Discovery.* Albany, N.Y.: State University of New York, 1988.

Hieronymus, Dr. T. "The E. E. Eeman Circuit," *Advanced Sciences Research and Development Advisory*. Lakemont, Georgia, July-August, 1986.

Hunt, R. *The Seven Keys to Color Healing: Diagnosis and Treatment Using Color*. San Francisco: Harper & Row, 1971.

Kaptchuk, T. *The Web That Has No Weaver*. N.Y.: Cogdon & Weed, 1983.

Kilner, W. *The Human Atmosphere; Or the Aura Made Visible by the Aid of Chemical Screens*. New York: Rebman, 1911.

Krieger, D. *The Therapeutic Touch: How to Use Your Hands to Help or to Heal*. Englewood Cliffs, N.J.: Prentice Hall, 1979.

Krippner, S., and D. Rubin (eds.). *Galaxies of Life: The Human Aura in Acupuncture and Kirlian Photography*. New York: Interface, 1973.

Lakhovsky, G. *The Secret of Life. Cosmic Rays and Radiations of Living Beings*. Translated from the French by Mark Clement. London: Heinemann, 1939.

Leadbeater, C. W. *The Chakras*. Wheaton, Ill.: Quest, Theosophical Publishing House, 1927.

Maby, J. C., and T. B. Franklin. *Physics of the Divining Rod*. London: B. Bell, 1939.

Manaka, Y., and K. Itaya. "Acupuncture as Intervention in the Biological Information System (Meridian Treatment and the X-signal System)." Unpublished article supplied by S. Birch.

Manaka, Y., and I. Urquart. *The Layman's Guide to Acupuncture*. New York and Tokyo: Weatherhill, 1972.

Mann, W. E. *Orgone, Reich and Eros*. New York: Simon & Schuster, 1973.

Matsumoto, K., and S. Birch. *Extraordinary Vessels*. Mass.: Paradigm, 1986.

Mesmer, F. A. *Mesmerism: A Translation of the Original Medical and Scientific Writings of F. A. Mesmer, M.D.*, compiled and translated by George J. Bloch, Ph.D. Los Altos, Calif.: William Kaufmann, 1980.

Nielsen, G., and J. Polansky. *Pendulum Power. A Mystery You Can See, a Power You Can Feel*. Rochester, Vermont: Destiny Books, 1987.

Powell, E. *Healing by Auto-Induction: Self-Healing While You Rest*. Sussex, England: Bruce Copen, no date.

_____ . *The Natural Home Physician. A Book for Every Household*. Essex, England: Health Science Press, 1981.

Reich, W. *The Bioelectric Investigation of Sexuality and Anxiety*. New York: Farrar, Straus and Giroux, 1982.

Reichenbach, K. von. *Physico-Physiological Researches on the Dynamics of Magnetism, Heat, Light, Electricity, and Chemism, in Their Relations to Vital Force*. New York: J. S. Redfield, 1851.

_____ . *The Odic Force: Letters on Od and Magnetism*. New Hyde Park, N.Y.: University Books, 1968.

Rhine, J. B. *Extra-Sensory Perception*. Boston: Bruce Humphries, 1934.

Richards, G. *The Chain of Life*. London: John Bale Sons and Danielsson, 1934.

Rothemich, A. "Sing the Body Electric," *The Laughing Man Magazine*, Vol. 6, No. 1: 45–47.

Russell, E. W. *Design for Destiny*. London: Neville Spearman, 1971.

_____ . *Report on Radionics: Science of the Future*. Suffolk: Neville Spearman, 1973.

Saraswati, Y. *Science of Soul*. Bharat: Yoga Niketan Trust, 1977.

_____ . *Science of Vital Force: A Treatise on Higher Yoga*. New Delhi: Yoga Niketan Trust, 1980.

Stark, E. *A History of Dowsing and Energy Relationships.* North Hollywood: BAC, 1978.

Stone, R. *Polarity Therapy: The Complete Collected Works.* Volumes 1 and 2. Reno, Nevada: CRCS Publications, 1987.

Swanholm, A. L. *The Brunler-Bovis Biometer and Its Uses.* Los Angeles: De Vorss, 1963.

Tansley, D. *Radionics and the Subtle Anatomy of Man.* Essex, England: Health Science Press, 1972.

_____. *Radionics: Science or Magic? An Holistic Paradigm of Radionic Theory and Practice.* Essex, England: C. W. Daniel, 1982.

Tiller, W. "Energy Fields and the Human Body, Part II," *A.R.E. Medical Symposium on Mind-Body Relationships in the Disease Process.* Phoenix, Arizona, January 1972.

_____. "Future Medical Therapeutics Based Upon Controlled Energy Fields," *Proceedings of the A.R.E. Medical Symposium.* Phoenix, Arizona, January 1976.

_____. "A Lattice Model of Space and Its Relationship to Multi-dimensional Physics," *Proceedings of the A.R.E. Medical Symposium.* Phoenix, Arizona, January 1977.

Tiller, W., and J. B. Carlton. "Positive-Negative Space/Time Energies," *Proceedings of the A.R.E. Medical Symposium.* Phoenix, Arizona, January 1977.

Tiller, W., and W. Cook. "Psychoenergetic Field Studies Using a Biomechanical Transducer. Part 1: Basics," *Proceedings of the A.R.E. Medical Symposium on New Horizons in Healing.* Phoenix, Arizona, January 1974.

Tompkins, P., and C. Bird. *The Secret Life of Plants.* New York: Harper & Row, 1973.

Watson, L. *Supernature.* London: Coronet Books, 1974.

Westlake, A. *The Pattern of Health.* New York: Devin-Adair Company, 1961.

_____. "Vis Medicatrix Naturae", *Proceedings of the Scientific and Technical Congress of Radionics and Radiesthesia.* London, May 16–18, 1950: 7–23. (Reprinted by Borderland Sciences Research Foundation, Garberville, Calif., 1987.)

Wolf, F. *Taking the Quantum Leap.* San Francisco: Harper & Row, 1981.

_____. *The Body Quantum. The New Physics of Body, Mind, and Health.* New York: Macmillan, 1986.

Index

References to figures, tables, and boxes are printed in boldface type.

Books That Transform Lives

WAY OF THE PEACEFUL WARRIOR
by Dan Millman
*"It may even change the lives of many . . .
who peruse its pages."*—DR. STANLEY KRIPPNER

**OPENING TO CHANNEL:
HOW TO CONNECT WITH YOUR GUIDE**
by Sanaya Roman and Duane Packer, Ph.D.
*This breakthrough book is the first
step-by-step guide to the art of channeling.*

TALKING WITH NATURE
by Michael J. Roads
*"From Australia comes a major new writer . . .
a magnificent book!"*—RICHARD BACH

CREATING MONEY
by Sanaya Roman and Duane Packer, Ph.D.
*The bestselling authors of OPENING TO CHANNEL
offer the reader the keys to abundance.*

SEEDS OF LIGHT
by Peter Rengel
*". . . contains a widely varied collection
of pearls of poetic wisdom."*—PROMETHEAN NETWORK

EAT FOR HEALTH
by William Manahan, M.D.
*"For those who care about their lives and bodies,
it will be a valuable resource."*—BERNARD S. SIEGEL, M.D.

H J Kramer Inc

Books That Transform Lives

THE EARTH LIFE SERIES
by Sanaya Roman, Channel for Orin

LIVING WITH JOY, BOOK I
"I like this book because it describes the way I feel about so many things."—VIRGINIA SATIR

PERSONAL POWER
THROUGH AWARENESS, BOOK II
"Every sentence contains a pearl. . . ."—LILIAS FOLAN

SPIRITUAL GROWTH, BOOK III
Orin teaches how to move to higher consciousness, link with the higher will, meet your higher self, and connect with the universal mind.

JOY IN A WOOLLY COAT
by Julie Adams Church
Destined to become a classic, JOY IN A WOOLLY COAT *is about living with, loving, and letting go of treasured animal friends.*

SINGING MAN
by Neil Anderson
"One of the finest allegories of our time . . . a story of everyman in transition."—JEAN HOUSTON

WAY OF THE PEACEFUL WARRIOR
An Audio Cassette
Read by Author Dan Millman
A 96-minute abridged version of the metaphysical classic, WAY OF THE PEACEFUL WARRIOR.

H J Kramer Inc

Biocircuit Resources

The best biocircuits are built of pure, quality materials. **Tools for Exploration** manufactures and sells the highest quality silk and copper biocircuits available—and for the price of a single massage! Below is a partial list of biocircuit tools and accessories offered by **Tools for Exploration**. Please write for a free catalog listing all available tools and accessories.

Copper Biocircuit—Elegantly crafted from copper screens, wires, and handles, with no toxic materials or attachments. This two-part biocircuit will form the Eeman general relaxation circuit. Package includes full instructions and a special audio tape with voice, music, and brain synchronization signals. **$39.95**

Silk Biocircuit—Constructed according to strict guidelines, of 100% silk and 100% cotton. This three-part biocircuit will form Eeman's two relaxation circuits or Lindemann's centrally symmetrical circuit. Includes full instructions and a unique audio tape with voice, music, and brain synchronization. **$49.95**

Cooperative Healing, by L. E. Eeman—Out of print for decades, Eeman's magnum opus has recently been reissued in its entirety by Health Research of Mokelumne Hill, CA, in a spiral-bound photocopy edition. **$30.00**

Order Form

QTY.	ITEM & DESCRIPTION	PRICE
	Copper Biocircuits (@ $39.95)	
	Silk Biocircuits (@ $49.95)	
	Eeman's *Cooperative Healing* (@ $30.00)	
	Total price of items	
	CA residents add 6% sales tax	
	Shipping & handling (UPS)	$ 3.50
	Special shipping (if applicable)	
	Total	$

Special Shipping:
1st class mail: *add* $3.50
2nd day air: *add* $4.00

Method of Payment:
Check or Money Order Enclosed ☐   Charge it to my: MasterCard ☐   Visa ☐
Credit Card Number (include all digits)   Exp. Date:

_____   _____

Signature as on card _____
                    (required for credit card purchases)

Your Name _____

Address _____

City _____ State _____ Zip _____

Day Phone (_____)_____
          (In case we have any questions about your order.)

Our Guarantee: Very simple. If for any reason you don't like your purchase, send it back undamaged for a prompt refund. Within 30 days, please.

Please make check payable to **Tools for Exploration**. Canadian and foreign orders payable in U.S. funds. Canadian and Mexican orders add $2.50 to U.S. postage; other foreign orders add $7.50 to U.S. postage. Regular orders will be shipped within 2 weeks of receipt. Special shipping will be shipped within 72 hours of receipt. Remember to allow time for UPS or other delivery after order is shipped. Incomplete orders will be returned.

Tools for Exploration
4286 Redwood Hwy. #C   San Rafael, CA 94903